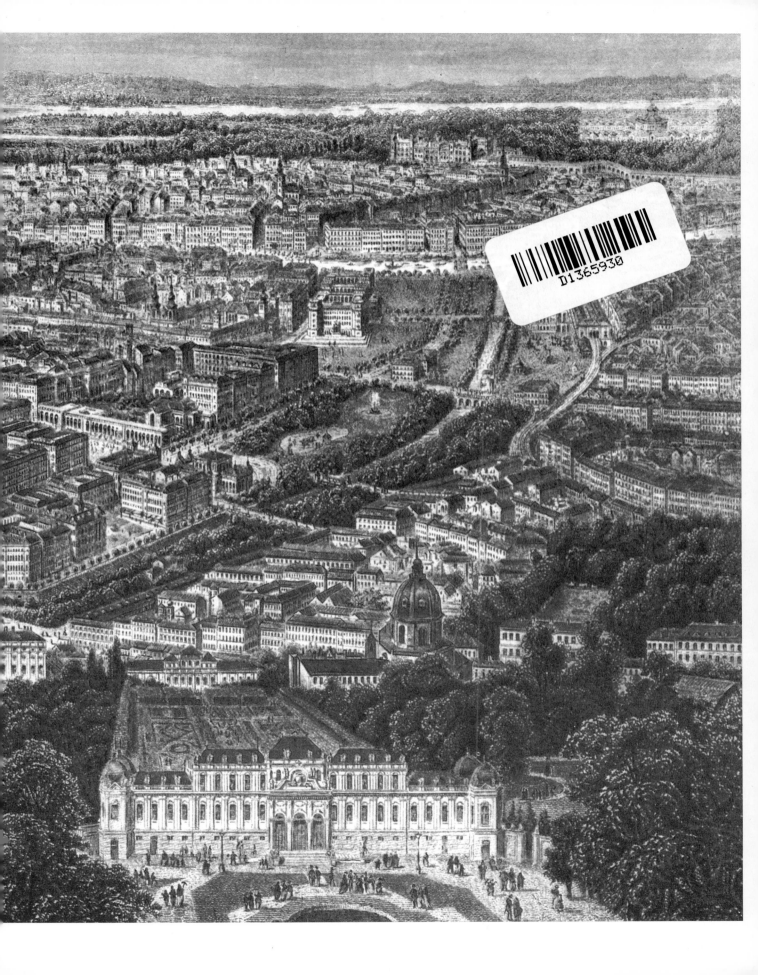

PETER PÖTSCHNER
VIENNA

VIENNA

TEXT: PETER PÖTSCHNER
INTRODUCTION: HELMUT ZILK
PHOTOGRAPHS BY HELLA PAWLOWSKI
ARRANGEMENT: JOCHEN PABST

PINGUIN-VERLAG, INNSBRUCK

English translation: Jacqueline Schweighofer

Photographs and picture agencies: Luftaufnahme Dr. Lothar Beckel (freige-
geben v. BMfLV mit Zl. 13088/200-1.6.88) 18/19; Lichtbildstelle des Bundes-
ministeriums für Land- und Forstwirtschaft 41b; Löbl-Schreyer 42/43,
44/45; Peter Mertz 50/51, 58a, 62a, 87u, 127d, 129b; Erik Pflanzer 31, 52a, b;
all other photographs by Hella Pawlowski.

Printing and binding: Druckerei Theiss GmbH, A-9400 Wolfsberg
Lithography: Ifolith, Innsbruck
Laserset: Josef Maringer, Maishofen
Printed in Austria
ISBN 3-7016-2317-1

FOREWORD

"Situated in the centre of southern Germany, this city of Vienna seems like a fount of light-heartedness and tranquillity amidst the earnest scientific and philosophical endeavours of neighbouring lands". That was how Auguste de la Garde, the French writer and man of letters, saw Vienna and the Viennese at the time of the Congress of Vienna. But this city is not solely associated with waltzing and wine and the countless ways of making life pleasant.

Far more, Vienna is one of the most ancient Central European settlements, a scene of history, a centre of commerce, a mediator between East and West. Favourably situated in the foothills of the Vienna Woods, at the intersection of major routes, Vienna passed through all the stages of a city on her long and laborious path.

A Roman fort, a border stronghold and a refuge from Germans, Huns and Avars, a trading post and a princely residence, a "bulwark of Christianity" in the face of the Turks, a centre of baroque architecture, the focal point and crucible of a multiracial state, the home of magnificent social reforms and, finally, the international UNO and Congress Centre, a tourist metropolis and a city which shows exemplary concern for environmental matters.

Foreign influences were absorbed and assimilated, from the rulers (Babenbergs, Habsburgs) and their retinues to the numerous peoples within the monarchy. Architecture, the fine arts, science, music, literature and the theatre profited from new ideas: the city was the birthplace of psychoanalysis, of the Viennese schools of medicine and music, and of much more besides. However much it might have changed in the course of the centuries, it has lost nothing of its magic. "Vienna remains Vienna" — despite opinions to the contrary, this is no threat, but a promise for the future!

Dr. Helmut Zilk
Former Mayor and Provincial Governor
of Vienna

CONTENTS

DISTRICTS

I. Innere Stadt
II. Leopoldstadt
III. Landstraße
IV. Wieden
V. Margareten
VI. Mariahilf
VII. Neubau
VIII. Josefstadt

IX. Alsergrund
X. Favoriten
XI. Simmering
XII. Meidling
XIII. Hietzing
XIV. Penzing
XV. Rudolfsheim-
    Fünfhaus

XVI. Ottakring
XVII. Hernals
XVIII. Währing
XIX. Döbling
XX. Brigittenau
XXI. Floridsdorf
XXII. Donaustadt
XXIII. Liesing

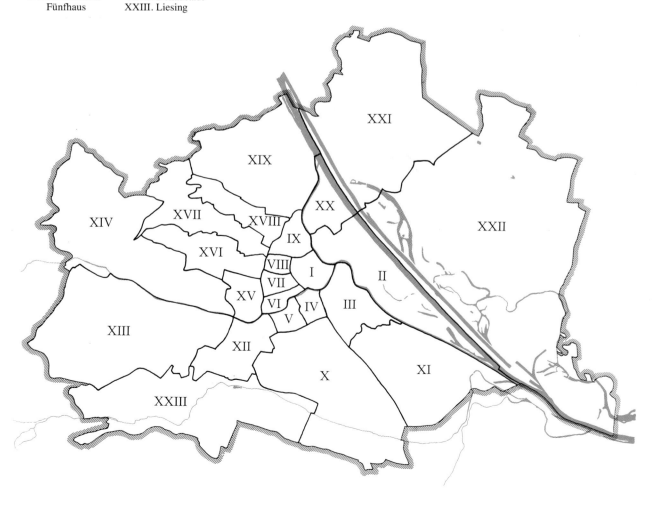

CHRONOLOGICAL TABLE

3rd millenium BC	Earliest established settlement of the Viennese area in the period of the (non-Indo-Germanic) Danubian culture.
2000—1200 BC	Immigration of northern farming peoples towards the end of the Neolithic Age.
1200—400 BC	Late Bronze Age migrations of Veneto-Illyrian tribes.
c. 400 BC	Celts subjugate the Illyrian population and establish the fortified settlement of Vindobona.
15 BC	Augustus occupies the Alpine region as far as the Danube. Noricum and the area of Vienna are Romanized.
Between AD 15 and 50	The former area of the Boii (deserta Boiorum) and the Viennese district go to the newly conquered province of Pannonia.
c. AD 90	The Ala Brittanica milliaria occupies a wooden auxiliary camp on the site of today's inner city.
Between 100 and 110	The 13th legion start to build a fortified camp and are relieved by the 14th legion who continue the work.
114	The 10th legion (Gemina pia fidelis) march into Vindobona.
167—180	During the Marcomanni offensive the camp and civilian settlement of Vindobona are overrun and plundered.
213	The civil town becomes a municipium.
c. 390	The notitia dignitatum, the late Roman state register, names Vindobona as the seat of the commander of the 10th legion and the port of the Danube fleet.
c. 400	The Marcomanni and the Quadi devastate Pannonia. Vindobona is sacked.
433	Theodosius II abandons Pannonia to the Huns.
488	Odoacer orders the return of the Roman population of Ufernoricum to Italy.
550	Jordanes mentions the Civitas Vindomina as a distant place in Hunnish Pannonia.
6th—8th century	Germanic peoples, Avars and Slavs leave their traces on Viennese soil. Findings in the most ancient part of the city indicate that the devastated Roman camp was again settled.
881	The Salzburg annals report the first conflict with incursive Hungarians at "Wenia".

976—1246 Babenberg rulers

1030	According to the Niederaltaich annals, Konrad II's army is taken captive by the Hungarians in or near "Wiennis".
1042	King Henry III holds court in Vienna.
1135	Margrave Leopold III the Holy breaks the might of the Sieghardings and Formbachs and becomes Governor of Vienna.
1137	Vienna is first called a town (civitas) in the Mauten contract of exchange.

1147	Consecration of the new Parish Church of St. Stephen.
1155	Heinrich II Jasomirgott founds the "Schottenkloster".
1156	Austria becomes a duchy. Heinrich II moves the Babenberg residence to Vienna.
1190	Walther von der Vogelweide, the minnesinger, comes to Vienna.
c. 1193	Duke Leopold V starts to build a ring wall around the enlarged city.
1220	Work commences on the second Romanesque building of St. Stephen's.
1221	Duke Leopold VI grants Vienna civic (and market) rights.
1237	After the banishment of Duke Frederick II the Quarrelsome, Emperor Frederick II proclaims the charter, making the city subject to the Emperor alone.
1247	After the death of the last Babenberg duke, Emperor Frederick II confirms the charter.

1251—1278 Vienna under Přemisl Ottocar, the Bohemian King.

1258, 1275	Devastating fires destroy large parts of the city.
c. 1275	Ottocar has a castle built by the "Widmertor", the origins of the "Hofburg".
1278	After the defeat and death of his adversary, Ottocar Přemisl, King Rudolf II enters Vienna. New civic rights: for a few years Vienna is again subject to the Emperor alone.

1281—1918 Habsburg rule

1282	First mention of a mayor of Vienna (Konrad Poll).
1288	A Viennese uprising against the stern rule of Albert I is suppressed. Loss of special rights.
1296	New charter (Albertinum I).
1304 (—1340)	The rebuilding of St. Stephen's Cathedral commences with the erection of the Albertine choir.
1316	Duke Frederick the Handsome presents Vienna with a Town Hall in the Salvatorgasse.
1326, 1327	In both years fires destroy vast parts of the city.
1340	Albert II the Lame codifies the civic rights.
1347	1,200 people die in an earthquake.
1349	The Black Death hits Vienna.
1359	Duke Rudolf IV the Founder lays the foundation stone of the nave of St. Stephen's.
1365	Rudolf the Founder establishes Vienna University.
1396	Albert IV and his brothers, Leopold and Wilhelm, alter the city charter: the Council is composed equally of hereditary citizens, merchants and artisans.
1408	After a Habsburg family quarrel, Konrad Vorlauf, the mayor, and two councillors are executed.
1410	Hans Giesser, a Hussite, is burnt at the stake.
1421	210 Viennese Jews are burnt at the stake in the presence of Duke Albert V and the populace.
c. 1422	Oldest plan of Vienna (Albertine Plan).
1433	The spire of St. Stephen's is completed.
1438	Oldest description of Vienna by Aeneas Silvius Piccolomini (later Pope Pius II).

Northern view of the city of Vienna, Michel Wolgemut, before 1493

1439	Albert V (II) has a bridge built across the Danube.
1440	Frederick III succeeds Albert II to the imperial throne. Vienna remains the seat of the Holy Roman Emperor until 1806 with few interruptions.
1450	The foundation stone is laid for the northern spire of St. Stephen's.
1451	Johannes Capistran, the Franciscan monk, preaches against the Turks.
1460	In the "Pancarta" Frederick III confirms all the rights and privileges granted by his predecessors.
1461	The twin-headed imperial eagle replaces the single-headed Babenberg eagle in Vienna's coat of arms.
1462	Supporters of Albert VI besiege Emperor Frederick III in the "Burg" from 21. 10. to 4. 12.
1463	Wolfgang Holzer, the mayor, is convicted of high treason and quartered.
1467	Stephen, the Waldensian bishop, is burnt at the stake.
1469	Vienna becomes a bishop's see.
1470	The oldest south view of Vienna and the first depiction of a Viennese street on two panels by the "Schottenmeister".
1485	Matthias Corvinus, the King of Hungary who had in 1477 vainly sought to take the city in a sudden attack, now enters in triumph after a long siege.
1490	Corvinus dies in the Hofburg at Vienna. Maximilian I repels the Hungarian occupation.
c. 1490	Oldest north view of Vienna in the Babenberg genealogical tree.
1497	Conrad Celtis founds the humanistic "Sodalitas literaria Danubiana".
1511	Work is interrupted on the north spire of St. Stephen's.
1515	Royal events in Vienna: Emperor Maximilian's grandchildren, Ferdinand and Maria are married to Anna and Ludwig, the children of Vladislav Jagiello, the King of Hungary and Bohemia.
1517	Maximilian I's city charter: Vienna loses its trading rights.
1522	Emperor Charles V cedes "rule in Austria" to Ferdinand, his brother, who takes up residence in Wiener Neustadt. On 11th April the mayor and

	five councillors are executed there after the abortive uprising of the estates in Vienna.
1524	Caspar Tauber, a Lutheran, is executed at the Stubentor.
1525	More than 400 houses and part of the suburbs are destroyed in the fire of 18th and 19th July.
1526	Ferdinand I's "city regulations" assign municipal administration to the sovereign authority.
1526 (—1565)	Construction of the Hernals water conduit.
1529	First Turkish siege from 22nd September to 20th October.

1531—1918 permanent seat of the Habsburg sovereigns and all court offices.

1531 (—1680)	Construction of the city fortifications, now reinforced by bastions and ravelins.
1546	The first history of the city, "Vienna Austria" by Wolfgang Lazius, is published in Basle. Establishment of the Municipal Guard to keep watch day and night at the gates and on the ramparts.
1547	The first trigonometrical plans of the city are produced by Augustin Hirschvogel and Bonifaz Wolmuet.
1551	The Jesuits under Petrus Canisius are called upon to carry out the Counter-Reformation.
1566	Survey of all citizens' houses for a court record of accommodation.
1577	Prohibition of Protestant church services.
1583	Elisabeth Pleichinger is burnt at the stake for witchcraft (the only witch-burning in Vienna).
1595	Count Hardegg is executed for surrendering Raab fortress to the Turks.
1598	Regulation of the Danube Canal.
1603	The new establishment of the Franciscan monastery inaugurates the "monastery offensive": religious orders found or rebuild numerous houses in the city and the suburbs.
1609	Jakob Hoefnagel draws the bird's-eye view of Vienna from the north.
1618	Emperor Matthias and Empress Anna found the imperial vault in the Capuchin monastery.

1618—1648 Thirty Years War

1619	The Prague insurgents, led by Matthias von Thurn, outside Vienna.
1623	Vienna University is handed over to the Jesuits.
1625	Part of the Unterer Werd is allotted to the Jews in order to build a ghetto.
1627	Last great fire in the city.
1645	The Swedes under Torstensson thrust forward to Vienna.
1663	After the loss of Neuhaeusel fortress, fear of the Turks grows in Vienna.
1670	Expulsion of the Jews from Vienna.
1679	The plague in Vienna.
1681	Folpert van Ouden-Allen draws the bird's-eye view of Vienna from the south.
1683	Second Turkish siege from 14th July to 12th September.

1686	Great building activity starts in the city and the suburbs: baroque Vienna begins to take shape.
1687	The first street lanterns are installed in the Dorotheergasse.
1693	The new Plague Column on the Graben is dedicated.
1695	Formation of the "Rumorwache", forerunners of the police.
1703	The "Wiennerische Diarium" (as from 1780 "Wiener Zeitung") is published for the first time on 8th August.
1704	After Kuruczen raids, bastions are built to protect the suburbs.
1709	Opening of the Kärntnertor Theatre.
1713	Plague in Vienna.
1716 (—1739)	The Karlskirche is built.
1726 (—1730)	The "Reichskanzlei" wing is added to the Hofburg.
1732	The cemetery outside the Cathedral is abandoned.
1739	Georg Raphael Donner's Providentia Fountain is re-erected in the "Mehlmarkt" (now the Neuer Markt).

1740—1790 The age of Maria Theresia and Joseph II.

1744	Foundation of the Porcelain Factory.
1752	Schönbrunn menagerie is founded.
1754	The first census in Vienna showed a population of 175,460.
1762	Mozart first comes to Vienna.
1766	The Prater is opened to the populace.
1769 (—1774)	Joseph Daniel Huber draws the large bird's-eye view of the city and all the suburbs, the plan being designed by Joseph Nagel.
1770	All Viennese houses are numbered for the first time.
1772	Introduction of the "Kleine Post" from door to door.
1773	Dissolution of the Jesuits.
1774	Introduction of general compulsory schooling.
1775	Free access to the Augarten.
1778	Streets in the old city are paved.
1781	Abolition of censorship, freedom of the press, the Patent of Toleration allows the Protestants freedom of worship.
1782	Dissolution of 18 Viennese monasteries. Pope Pius VI visits Vienna.
1783	Reorganization of the Municipal Authority: the *Magistrat* is constituted.
1784	Opening of the General Hospital.
1786	First performance of Mozart's *The Marriage of Figaro* in the old Burgtheater.
1787	Opening of the "Freihaustheater auf der Wieden".
1788	Opening of the "Theater in der Josefstadt".
1791	Blanchard flies from the Prater to Gross-Enzersdorf in his balloon.

1792—1815 Austria at war with France.

1792	Beethoven comes to Vienna.

1795	The building of new factories is prohibited. Jacobin trials in Vienna.
1798	First performance of Haydn's *The Creation* in the Schwarzenberg Palace on the Neuer Markt.
1801	Opening of the "Theater an der Wien".
1803	Wiener Neustadt Canal goes into use. Construction of Albertine water conduit.
1804	Emperor Francis II is proclaimed Francis I, Emperor of Austria.
1805	The French outside Vienna: the city is surrendered without fighting on 13. 11. First performance of Beethoven's *Fidelio* in the "Theater an der Wien" on 20. 11.
1807	Adolf Bäuerle founds the "Theaterzeitung".
1809	Austria alone at war with France. 10th May: Napoleon in Schönbrunn. The city capitulates after two days' bombardment. Death of Haydn.
1811	National bankruptcy: banknotes reduced to one fifth of their value.
1812	Foundation of the "Gesellschaft der Musikfreunde".
1814 (—1815)	The Congress of Vienna.
1815	Foundation of the Polytechnic (now the Technical University).
1816	Archduchess Henriette, the wife of Archduke Karl, introduces Vienna to the Christmas tree.
1825	The first omnibus starts operating on the Vienna-Hietzing route.
1827	Beethoven's death.
1828	Schubert's death.
1829	Foundation of the Danube Steamship Company.
1830	The Danube floods.
1831	Cholera in Vienna: 20,000 deaths.
1834	First performance of Ferdinand Raimund's "Verschwender" in the "Theater in der Josefstadt".
1837	The "Nordbahn" starts running on the Floridsdorf — Deutsch-Wagram line.
1842	Otto Nicolai founds the Philharmonic Concerts.
1845	First gas lanterns in streets and squares.
1848	Revolution in Vienna. Bombardment and storming of the city in October.

1848—1916 The age of Francis Joseph I.

1850	Provisional by-laws. The suburbs as far as the bastions become part of the municipality. Vienna has 431,000 inhabitants.
1852	Public Council Meetings are prohibited.
1857	The fortifications are abandoned and demolished between 1858 and 1876.
1861	Free council elections again and municipal self-administration.

1861—1896 Liberals hold the council majority

1862	The Danube floods.
1865	Opening of the first section of the Ringstrasse.
1867	First performance of Johann Strauss' *Blue Danube* waltz.
1869	Opening of the Court Opera House.
1870 (—1873)	Construction of the first water conduit fed from high altitude springs.

1870 (—1875)	Regulation of the Danube.
1873	World Exhibition — Stock Exchange crashes — cholera epidemic. Joseph Schöffel prevents sale and deforestation of the Vienna Woods.
1874	The Central Cemetery is consecrated.
1881	"Ringtheater" fire.
1883	The steam tramway starts operating on the Hietzing-Perchtoldsdorf route.
1885	First Council Meeting in the new Town hall.
1890	Removal of the bastions; further suburbs become part of the municipality. Vienna numbers 1,365,548 inhabitants.

1895—1919 Christian Socialist council majority

1896	Opening of the first cinema in Vienna. The "Stadtbahn" is inaugurated.
1897	First electric tram-line.
1899	The municipal gasworks are opened.
1900	The 20th District, Brigittenau, is formed by dividing the 2nd District.
1902	Completion of the Municipal Electricity Works. Electrification of the tramway.
1904	Floridsdorf incorporated in the municipality as 21st District.
1905	Creation of the green belt.
1910	Completion of the second water conduit fed from high altitude springs. Vienna numbers 2,031,498 inhabitants.
1913	Count Zeppelin lands in Vienna in his airship.

1914—1918 First World War

1918	Proclamation of the Republic. Vienna becomes the Federal Capital.

1919—1934 Social Democratic majority on the Council

1919	Lainz Zoo is opened to the public.
1920	Municipal statutes and municipal election regulations are renewed, Vienna acquires a new constitution.
1921	The first Viennese Trade Fair is held.
1922	Vienna becomes a Federal Province.
1923	Introduction of housing tax. Major communal housing programme.
1925	Electrification of the "Stadtbahn".
1927	Unrest in Vienna; Palace of Justice set on fire.
1931	Opening of the Prater Stadium.
1934	February battles. Prohibition of the Social Democratic Party and dissolution of the Municipal Council.

1934—1938 Authoritarian "Corporative State"

1934	July *putsch* by the National Socialists.
1935	Opening of the Höhenstrasse.
1937	Rotunda fire in the Prater.
1938	After the incorporation of Austria in the German Reich, 97 border communes in Lower Austria are included in the formation of "Greater Vienna" (with 26 districts).
1939	Vienna becomes a "Reichsgau".

1939—1945 Second World War

1944	As from April, air raids on Vienna.
1945	21. 2. and 12. 3. Air raids cause much destruction.
	2. 4. Vienna becomes a battle area.
	12. 4. St. Stephen's Cathedral fire.
	13. 4. The Red Army enters the city.
	27. 4. Proclamation of the Second Republic. Restoration of democratic conditions. The Allies divide the city into four zones of occupation.

As from 1945 Socialist majority on the Council

1948	Consecration of the rebuilt St. Stephen's Cathedral.
1951	The first Festival of Vienna.
1954	Separation of 80 Lower Austrian communes. Vienna has 23 districts.
1955	State Treaty. Withdrawal of occupation troops. Opening of the restored State Opera House.
1956	Vienna becomes the seat of the International Atomic Energy Agency.
1961	J. F. Kennedy and N. S. Krushchev meet in Vienna.
1964	Vienna numbers 1,635,700 inhabitants.
1967	The UNIDO headquarters are based in Vienna.
1969	Work commences on the underground.
1972 (—1987)	Construction of the relief watercourse (New Danube).
1979	Opening of the Vienna International Centre (UNO City).
1987	Opening of the Austria Center Vienna.
1990	"Round Table" on a Danube boat in Vienna with the new democratic leadership in the Central European reform countries.
1993	Fire in the "Redoutensaal" of the Hofburg in Vienna.
1996	For the first time the SPÖ fails to obtain an absolute majority in Viennese council elections.
1996	International Theodor-Herzl-Symposium in Vienna.
1997	Opening of Freudenau power station.
2000	Completion of the Millennium Tower in Vienna, Austria's highest building (202 m).

THE INNER CITY
AND THE
RINGSTRASSE ZONE

Vienna's early development was marked by the building of Vindobona, the legionary camp which was constructed in around 100 BC in place of an older Roman cavalry camp at the northern boundary of the Roman Empire. Its outline is still distinguishable on the city plan of today: it corresponded to the square formed by the Tiefer Graben, Naglergasse — Graben, Kramergasse — Rotgasse and the steep slope down to the Danube Canal. The Schottengasse — Herrengasse — Augustinerstrasse roads indicate the course taken by the *limes;* this ran past the camp. Abandoned in around 400 in the turmoils of the *Völkerwanderung,* the legionary camp was plundered and destroyed, but it is now presumed that the ruins were still populated, albeit sparsely. Various old settlement forms dating back to the high Middle Ages can be made out within the borders of the former Roman camp: in the southern section, next to the former *porta decumana,* was the "Reststadt", a clustered village with the Church of St. Peter; the fortified church settlement at the northern edge was somewhat younger, perhaps dating back to the 9th century. Probably enlarged during the 11th century, the settlement adjoined the "Reststadt" and took the shape — still retained in the Tuchlauben and side streets — of an alley-grouped village, forming the centre of the triangular area at the fork of the Tuchlauben and the Kühfussgasse. The hamlet-like settlement around the Church of "Maria am Gestade" also dates back to the 11th century and was built on top of Roman remains.

Small trading settlements developed along the eastern and southern exit roads in front of the walls of the former Roman camp. One of these was the "Hungarian suburb" between Lugeck and Ignaz Seipel-Platz or the suburb outside the Peilertor, later the Kohlmarkt. In around 1137 construction work started on the new Parish Church of St. Stephen. In 1156 Vienna became a palatinate of the Babenbergs. Heinrich Jasomirgott founded the "Schottenkloster" next to the ducal residence Am Hof and this led to the settlement of the area in the immediate proximity of the former *limes.* Towards the end of the 12th century the ditch surrounding the Roman camp was levelled out and a new system of parallel alleys was laid out between the Kohlmarkt and the Spiegelgasse. A similar network developed to the east of the Kärntner Strasse. At the same time the town wall was extended, remaining unchanged until 1857. In the 13th century the merged settlements were enlarged, rectangular areas being laid out. It was then that the Graben, Hoher Markt, Neuer Markt and Judenplatz — later the centre of the ghetto — took shape. The ruler's residence and castle on the southern edge of the city probably date back to Ottocar II Premisl. The town's development — affluence had come with trading on the Danube — was furthered by the building of various monasteries during the 13th century; the Order of the Holy Ghost already owned a hospital in front of the Kärntnertor in 1211.

Essentially, the city has retained the layout it acquired in around 1300. Vienna's modern history was largely determined by its conversion into one of Europe's most impregnable strongholds and its elevation to an imperial residence. The mediaeval buildings were gradually renewed, particularly after the victory over the Turks, this providing tremendous impetus. The Josefsplatz and Dr. Ignaz Seipel-Platz were both added during the baroque era.

During the late 18th century Vienna started to develop into a big modern city. Large dwelling houses were erected in the inner city.

Subsequently, during the great building era in the second half of the 19th century, most of the inner city houses were rebuilt. Long deferred, work on demolishing the fortifications commenced in 1858. The glacis land was converted into building land and the Ringstrasse was laid out. This concept of a total work of art gave its name to an entire epoch, historicism, and it constitutes the last inner city development on a grand scale.

From time immemorial the Stephansplatz has been the real centre of Vienna. It is dominated by St. Stephen's Cathedral; this acquired its present appearance in the mid-16th century after centuries of building. The row of houses opposite the Riesentor originally dated back to 19th century historicism. Destroyed in 1945, the buildings were replaced in the Fifties. The other house groups here grew up in the course of the centuries, the oldest being the Deutsche Haus and the Archbishop's Palace. Decorated with armorial devices, the main facade of the bishop's residence dominates the top part of the Rotenturmstrasse. Branching off from this road is the Wollzeile, its character predominantly 18th century and Biedermeier; the narrow courtyard passage through to the Lugeck is particularly delightful. Behind the Cathedral, in the area between the Schulerstrasse and the Singerstrasse, are narrow, winding lanes with modest baroque houses. The top part of the Singerstrasse is characterized by the baroque front of the house of the Teutonic Order; further down are various artistic and historically significant 17th and 18th century buildings, adding an ornamental touch to the road. The winding course taken by the Wollzeile is an indication of its great age; dating back to different epochs, the houses here form a harmonious group. The Franziskanerplatz is dominated by the post-Gothic gabled front of the Franciscan Church and the adjoining monastery building with its unusual window decoration. The Moses fountain was erected here in 1798 by Johann Martin Fischer. A passageway in the neo-classical house at number 5

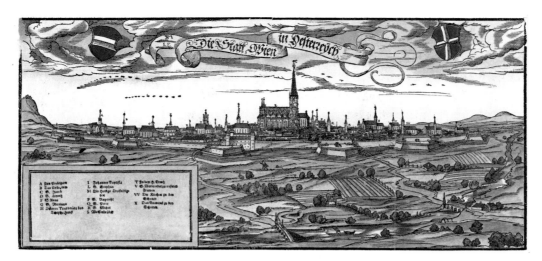

Vienna, Chronique
de Nürenberg, 1493

leads to the narrow, winding Ballgasse. An elongated square open on all sides, the Graben was probably created in around 1190 when the ditch of the Roman camp was levelled out; in mediaeval days its eastern edge was built on to the Roman camp wall which was still preserved in parts. According to legend, the nearby Church of St. Peter was founded by Charlemagne. The old church had to give way to Hildebrandt's magnificent domed edifice in around 1700. The Graben quickly became a major east-west connection, a market square and the site of representational events. In 1687 the Trinity Column was erected, a vow having been made to this effect in the Plague year of 1679 by Emperor Leopold I. It was a combined work by notable sculptors. In their present form, the fountains at each side with the statues of Sts. Leopold and Joseph date back to 1804. Today, the Graben's characteristic appearance derives from its almost total renewal in the 19th century, when it became an elegant street of shops. It runs straight into the Stock-im-Eisen-Platz which acquired its name from the ancient symbol on a corner of the palace in this square.

Grand late 19th century shop premises also dominate the Kärntner Strasse; of the older buildings only the little Esterhazy Palace and the Malteserkirche with its new neo-classical facade remain. The Kärntner Strasse is a pedestrian zone, this

lending a very special touch. Baroque buildings predominate in the side streets. Distinctive monumental buildings abound: J. B. Fischer von Erlach's and Lukas von Hildebrandt's winter palace for Prince Eugene (now the Ministry of Finance), the Palais Fürstenberg in the Himmelpfortgasse, the Questenberg and Schoeller Palaces, the Savoy Convent, the Court Archives (with Grillparzer's study), the Ursuline Convent with its gabled church front (now the Academy of Music and the Arts), the Church of St. Anne and several imposing patrician houses in the Annagasse. The Krugerstrasse and the Walfisch-gasse in the area adjoining the Ringstrasse mainly feature 19th century buildings, but the line of the mediaeval city wall can still be made out at the top of the Walfischgasse in the conspicuous curve of houses 5 to 9.

In the bend of the Ringstrasse by the former Schottentor two old main roads branch off, the Alser Strasse and the Währinger Strasse. Broadening into a square, the newer part of the Schottengasse ist distinguished by Theophil Hansen's block of buildings at 9-11 (formerly the Palais Ephrussi) and the monumental stone facade of the Creditanstalt which was completed in 1924. The sudden narrowing of the Schottengasse reveals the site of the city gate, demolished in 1862. Remains of the fortifications still exist in the neighbouring Mölkerbastei, the

old buildings here including the Pasqualatihaus at no. 8, where Beethoven lived. The older section of the Schottengasse is characterized by Josef Kronhäusel's Schottenhof and the late baroque Melkerhof. With its unusual layout and its buildings of artistic and historic note, the Freyung is one of Vienna's most impressive squares. In the narrow Herrengasse — this was mentioned as early as 1216 — one edifice of significance adjoins the next, administrative buildings, noble's palaces and imposing 19th and 20th century banking houses forming a complex of historic dimensions. The same can be said of the parallel Wallnerstrasse with its row of palaces in the style of baroque and classicism. Bounded by the Löwelstrasse and the Herrengasse, the governmental quarter is also rich in baroque palaces, once the residence of aristocratic families, now official buildings. The Minoritenplatz is dominated by the Gothic Minoritenkirche with its pitched roof and its slender octagonal spire. Built between 1717 and 1719 according to plans by Lukas von Hildebrandt, the Federal Chancellery forms a funnel-shaped square with the Amalienburg opposite.

The Hofburg group comprises the Burg itself, the National Library, both court theatres (State Opera House and Burgtheater), the museums, court stables (now the trade fair site) and the former court churches of St. Augustine and St. Michael. The

Hofburg's long development probably commenced in the era of Ottocar II Premisl with the building of a citadel. The tournament ground was rebuilt after the 16th century, the Amalienburg dating back to 1575, the Leopoldine Wing to 1660 and the magnificent State Chancellery to 1726. The domed Michaeler Wing was not added until 1893. In the 18th century the area between the Schweizerhof and the Augustine monastery was rebuilt on a generous scale, the Josefsplatz and Fischer von Erlach's library dating back to this period. Jean-Nicolas Jadot de Ville-Issey's and Nikolaus Pacassi's wings were added somewhat later. With its harmonious proportions and its magnificent architecture, this square is astounding in its effect.

The east side of the Michaelerplatz is defined by the neo-classical facade of the Michaelerkirche and its slender Gothic spire. The magnificent front of the Hofburg opposite contrasts strangely with Adolf Loos' facade for the Goldmann & Salatsch shop. Completed in 1910, this provoked a storm of indignation. The Kohlmarkt leading up to the Michaelertor of the Hofburg is characterized by elegant residential and business premises. A narrow passage, the Michaeler Durchgang, provides a view of the chancel and side of the Michaelerkirche and leads to the Habsburgergasse. Baroque houses and palaces and Biedermeier housing alternate with noble apartment houses with up to seven storeys. The neo-baroque facade of Gottlieb Nigelli's Protestant Church in the Dorotheergasse can be seen from afar.

First mentioned in 1234, the Neue Markt is attached to this network of roads. Here, immediately adjoining the Kärntner Strasse, a trading centre with the south developed in mediaeval days. Grain and flour were major commodities, which is how it came to be called the Mehlmarkt. In 1739 Georg Raffael Donner's Providentia Fountain was installed here. An

unbroken row of baroque houses has been preserved along the west side next to the Capuchin Church, famous for its imperial vaults.

The Tegetthoffstrasse connecting the Neue Markt with the Albertinaplatz took shape in 1883 after the demolition of an old hospital; the Albrechtsrampe, the last remains of an ancient bastion, gives it a dramatic touch. The tapering building complex of the Augustine Monastery and Archduke Albrecht's former palace —this houses the famous Albertina graphic collections — finds a dramatic conclusion in the equestrian statue of this archduke. The lower section is decorated with the remains of the 19th century fountain. In the immediate vicinity, the early baroque Lobkowitz palace is of note and the view of the Augustinerstrasse is impressive. The church which dominates this road contains the tomb of Archduchess Marie Christine von Canova.

In the south-west quarter of the old Roman camp are two high mediaeval squares: Am Hof is dominated by the magnificent baroque facade of the Church of Nine Choirs of Angels, the baroque column of the Virgin Mary (1666) and the imposing lines of the old arsenal building, now the fire brigade headquarters, whereas the Judenplatz is characterized by a group of old Viennese houses and the rear of the former Bohemian Court Chancellery, completed in 1754.

The narrow streets in this area have retained much of their old town atmosphere. The baroque houses are in essence Gothic, some of them with picturesque gables. In the Wipplingerstrasse the Bohemian Court Chancellery and the Alte Rathaus have both been preserved, the latter featuring an elaborately arranged baroque facade. Since 1871 the Gothic Chapel of the Saviour has served the Old Catholics. The quarter surrounding the late Gothic Church of Maria am Gestade — the spire was completed in 1430 — still abounds in old build-

Vienna and the suburbs in the first half of the 18th

14

...ntury, steel engraving by Matthäus Seutter

ings, some dating back to the 16th century.

The Hohe Markt, one of Vienna's oldest squares, was a centre of urban life well into the 19th century. After major bomb damage the only reminders of its former significance are Fischer von Erlach's fountain (1732) and Franz Matsch's clock (1913) with its daily parade at noon of life-sized statues of historical figures. The area around St. Ruprecht dates back to Vienna's beginnings, although the houses are mainly early 19th century. Their simple facades provide a foil for the Romanesque church, the oldest place of worship in the city. Dignified residential and business premises dating back to the beginning of this century adorn the Fleischmarkt. A charming contrast is provided by a picturesque complex of old Viennese houses where the Hafnersteig runs into the Fleischmarkt. This is also the site of Theophil Hansen's brickwork Greek Orthodox Church of the Holy Trinity which was built in 1858. With its narrow streets and its almost entirely Renaissance and baroque buildings, the old quarter of town between the Fleischmarkt and the Wollzeile constitutes one of the most impressive inner city ensembles. Hidden amongst residential buildings is the delightful Heiligenkreuzerhof, its simplicity highlighted by the decorated baroque portico of the prelates' wing. The rows of houses in the Köllnerhofgasse, Schönlaterngasse, Sonnenfelsgasse and Bäckerstrasse consist mainly of patrician buildings dating back to the 16th to 18th century. They feature ornate facades, porches decorated with armorial bearings or sculpture work, and inner courtyards which exude atmosphere. The tiny Dr. Ignaz Seipel-Platz (formerly the Universitätsplatz) was created in c. 1630 when the University Church was built. It acquired its magnificent baroque interior in around 1705, the work of Andrea Pozzo. The severe facade of the

church with its twin spires and the economic arrangement of the front of the former Jesuit College contrast delightfully with the magnificent late baroque auditorium (now the Academy of Science) by Jean Nicolas Jadot de Ville-Issey. The spreading complex of the old University is adjoined by the administrative buildings of the Postal Authority, some of which were originally monastery buildings. Essentially baroque, the main post office was redecorated by Paul Sprenger in 1851 and forms a barrier between the old part of the city and the Ringstrasse.

The central section of the Postgasse is bordered to the east by the richly arranged facade of the Dominican Church and by the remains of the Dominican monastery which was restored in the 17th century. Behind the main Post Office is Otto Wagner's world-famous Post Office Savings Bank. The huge government building in the Stubenring opposite was once the Imperial War Ministry and was built according to plans by Ludwig Baumann, its historicism being sufficiently imperial for the Ringstrasse.

The Dr. Karl Lueger-Platz with Josef Müllner's monument to that mayor of Vienna provides a transition from the buildings erected on the Parkring between 1860 and 1880 to the blocks on the Stubenring, built at the beginning of this century. As the road narrows to join the Wollzeile, the site of the old Stubentor can be made out. Designed by Heinrich Ferstel in the Italian Renaissance style, the Academy of Applied Arts, originally the Austrian Museum of Art and Industry, was the first building (1871) on the Stubenring. It remained solitary for some time. The extension in the Weiskirchnerstrasse was built between 1960 and 1908 according to plans by Ludwig Baumann.

The buildings in the Vordere Zollamtsstrasse — it accompanies the final section of the right bank of the Wien — have a monumental character.

Public and private buildings dating back to around 1900 adjoin the long front of Paul Sprenger's Fiscal Headquarters building. They include the former Royal and Imperial Admiralty which bears the coats of arms of all the ports in the Habsburg Empire. The spacious arrangement of the river Wien, with numerous bridges, the railway line and the imposing government building on the other side, all give this area an urban, boulevard-like character.

Numerous representational buildings line the Parkring and the Schubertring. The former palace of the Master of the Teutonic Order is of particular note and was designed by Theophil Hansen. With its wider roads and larger plots of land, the area of the city that was extended during the late 19th century contrasts markedly with the old city. The Himmelpfortgasse-Seilerstätte junction is dominated by the monumental corner with the old Stadttheater, later the Ronacher. The Palais Coburg in the Seilerstätte was built between 1843 and 1849.

Now surrounded by modern, palatial hotels, the Stadtpark was designed by Josef Selleny, the landscape painter, and laid out by Rudolf Sieböck, the landscape gardener. It was opened in 1862. In the course of the years various monuments were erected there. The Kursalon was built between 1865 and 1867 according to plans by Johann Garben. When the river Wien was built up in 1903, its banks acquired a pleasing arrangement of promenades, stairways and sculptural decorations. Designed in the spirit of art nouveau, these grounds culminate in the river portal, a semicircular arrangement flanked by domed pavilions and having wide steps, interspersed with pylons and walls. It continues as far as the Johannesgasse, where it harmonizes with Otto Wagner's Stadtbahn station. In the centre of the nearby Beethovenplatz is the statue of the composer by Kaspar Zumbusch, it was unveiled in 1880. The southern side is taken up by the neo-Gothic, brickwork Akademisches Gymnasium (1863) by Friedrich Schmidt. The Konzerthaus and the Academy of Music were erected opposite in 1910. The Schwarzenbergplatz developed in two phases: the section nearer to the city, with the equestrian statue of Field Marshal Prince Carl zu Schwarzenberg by Ernst Julius Hähnel, absolutely exemplifies severe historicism. The southern section, on the other hand — it did not develop until the first decade of this century — displays the typical features of late historicism. The rounded corners of the mighty, stone-dressed building blocks lead across to the fork of the Prinz Eugen-Strasse and the Rennweg. The French Embassy building provides a conspicuous contrast to this architecture. Designed by Georg-Paul Chedanne, it is a characteristic work of French art nouveau. The fountain (1873) and the Russian memorial (1945) accentuate the central axis of this urban area which is impressively rounded off by the Palais Schwarzenberg in the south.

Before the fortifications were demolished, the Karlsplatz was a swamp beside the river. In the early 18th century it acquired a commanding focal point — the Karlskirche, that magnificent creation by both Fischer von Erlachs with frescos and paintings by Rottmayr, Gaetano Fanti and Daniel Gran, sculptures by Mattielli, and Corradini and works by many other artists. The Polytechnic was built next to the Karlskirche between 1816 and 1818, the forerunner of today's Technical University. When the Ringstrasse was laid out and the river Wien redirected at the end of the century, the scene gradually took shape. Of the buildings on the city side, part of the Ringstrasse zone, the Handelsakademie (Ferdinand Fellner sen., 1860—1862), the Künstlerhaus (August Weber, 1865—1868) and the Musikverein (Theophil Hansen, 1867—1869) are of particular artistic and cultural note. The western side of

the Karlsplatz was not concluded until much later when the Sezession (Joseph M. Olbrich, 1897—1898) and the Austrian Travel Office (Heinrich Schmid and Hermann Aichinger, 1923) were built.

The Kärntnerring and the Opernring date back to the 1860s and are thus two of the oldest sections of the Ringstrasse. In this area a specific architectural form was developed for purpose-built blocks of flats, the unity of the whole block being of prime importance, but the individual unit nevertheless retaining some independence. The Court Opera House, now the State Opera House, was designed by August Sicardsburg and Eduard van der Nüll and was completed in 1869, the first monumental building on the Ringstrasse. It is situated at the main exit of old Vienna, in the area of the old Kärntnertor. On the outer edge of the extended city zone is the Schillerplatz; in its regularity a fine example of severe historicism, it is the site of Theophil Hansen's Academy of Art (1872/76). The memorials to Goethe and Schiller reflect that epoch's cult of monuments.

The fall of the bastions meant that the Hofburg could be extended on a lavish scale. Planned by Gottfried Semper and Carl Hasenauer, the "imperial forum" was meant to link the Neue Burg and the Court Museums in one complex, but it was never finished. Forming a wide exedra, the sweeping south wing of the Neue Burg now stands alone at the end of the Heldenplatz. On the other side of the Ringstrasse the powerful, domed stone facades of the museums impressively screen a park-like square, its focal point the monument to Maria Theresia. The south-west conclusion of this area is formed by the elongated front of the court stables which were designed by Fischer von Erlach the elder. Both the Burggarten and the Volksgarten occupy the site of older gardens which once lay within the shadow of

the fortifications. High railings still shield the Hofburg area and the gardens from the Ringstrasse.

Like the court stables, the western row of the Auerspergstrasse was a part of the "glacis front", the facades of the Palais Auersperg and Fischer von Erlach's Palais Trautson providing the main artistic accent. The gap between the court stables and the Palais Trautson is taken up by the Volkstheater (1887) and Franz Vogl's monument to Ferdinand Raimund originally stood in front of this, but was moved in 1938. The elegant Palais Epstein was built according to Theophil Hansen's plans in 1870. The Parliament building just near was erected between 1874 and 1884. Long regarded as Hansen's major work, it is ingeniously planned down to the smallest detail: even the Athene fountain was created to the architect's design. Between these buildings is the park-like Schmerlingplatz, screened from the road behind by the Palace of Justice. The latter's original appearance underwent considerable changes after the fire in 1927.

The spaciously designed area around Friedrich von Schmidt's Town Hall (1873/83) took shape within a decade. Designed by architects of note, the stylish blocks of flats are accentuated by tower-like structures at the corners and are arcaded on one side, giving this area an urban unity.

The adjoining Dr. Karl Lueger-Ring provides a highlight thanks to its architectural and urban planning, combining monumental buildings like the University (1873—1883) and the Burgtheater (1874—1888) with spacious gardens. Ferstel's neo-Gothic Votivkirche (1856/79) is integrated in this concept. The focal point of the adjoining area to the west is Theophil Hansen's Stock Exchange building (1868/74). Of the residential buildings on the Schottenring, Otto Wagner's design for no. 23 is particularly remarkable with its polychrome facade.

Step by step the ancient church of Maria am Gestade is revealed. Built at the edge of the fortified city, high above the Danube, it was frequently destroyed and again restored

Page: 18/19:
Aerial view of the city centre: the outline of Vindobona, the Roman camp, can still be distinguished

St. Stephen's Cathedral:
a) Know as "Steffl", the lofty south tower is Vienna's most famous feature,
b) View from St. Stephen's Cathedral across the rooftops of the inner city towards the Votivkirche and the new complex of the General Hospital
c) The pulpit is a masterpiece of Anton Pilgram
d) Virgin Mary, c. 1325, the oldest Marian sacred image in the Cathedral

a

b

c

d

Page 24
South roof of the
Cathedral nave with
Gothic gables, finials and
pinnacles

St. Stephen's Cathedral is
reflected in the facade of
the "Haas-Haus"
(Hans Hollein 1990)

Fiacre at Stephansplatz

Page 28:
Rooftops in the old city; in the front, the courtyard of the house of the Teutonic Order in the Stephansplatz

Page 29:
In the Schönlaterngasse

The inscription on the Plague Column reads:

TIBI REGIS OECULORUM IMMORTALI:
UNI IN ESSENTIA ET TRINO IN PERSONIS,
DEO:
INFINITE BONO, ÆTERNO ET IMMENSO,
CUIUS DEXTERÆ OMNIA SUNT POSSIBILIA,
CUIUS SAPIENTIÆ NIHIL EST ABSCONDITUM,
CUIUS PROVIDENTIA SUA DISPOSITIONE
NON FALLITUR,
CUIUS POTESTATE IMPLETUR UNIVERSUM,
CUIUS MISERICORDIA SUPER OMNIA OPERA,

Page 30:
a) The Graben: dating back to a vow made in 1679, the Plague Column was completed in 1962; in the front, the Leopold Fountain
b) An unusual scene: a flurry of early-morning snow in the almost deserted Kohlmarkt.

Page 31:
On the base of the Plague Column: Emperor Leopold I in prayer. – The plague, overcome by faith. Figures by Paul Strudel, reliefs by Ignaz Bendl

Page 32/33:
Stephansplatz, "Haas-Haus" (a) – Pedestrian zone in the Kärntner Strasse (b, d) – Hotel Sacher (c)

c

d

In the Kohlmarkt:
a) Shop doorway by
Hans Hollein
b, c) Cafe Demel

b

c

Andromeda Fountain in
the courtyard of the Alte
Rathaus, Wipplinger
Strasse 8, by Georg
Raphael Donner

Fountain by Joseph
Emanuel Fischer von
Erlach and Antonio
Corradini in the Hohe
Markt

Georg Raphael Donner's
Providentia Fountain in
the Neue Markt

Am Hof: putti on the base
of the Column of the
Virgin Mary, restored in
1667 by Balthasar Herold.
At the back, an allegorical
group by Lorenzo Mattielli
on the attic storey of the
former Arsenal (now the
fire brigade headquarters)

a) Monument to Emperor Josef II by Franz Anton Zauner in the Josefsplatz; at the back, the central pavilion of the National Library; the quadriga on the attic storey is by Lorenzo Mattielli
b) Main facade of the Landhaus in the Herrengasse. On the right, the former Bank and Stock Exchange building by Heinrich Ferstel; the Cafe Central on the ground floor
c) The Augustinerbastei with the main facade of the Albertina (formerly Duke Albert of Saxe-Teschen's palace)
d) View of the Neue Burg; to the right, the back of the National Library
e) Monument to Archduke Albrecht by Kaspar Zumbusch. To the right, the back of the Opera House

b

a) The arcades of the Stallburg
b) Lipizzaners being led to their stables
c) Hofburg, Schweizertor: armorial bearings and inscription of King Ferdinand I, 1552

FERDINAN GERMAN BOEM ZC HISP ARC DVX BVR ANNO

DVS ROM HVNGAR REX INFA HI AVSTR GVND ZC M D LII

c

41

a) Hofburg, Franz Joseph's
apartment, the Emperor's
study
b) Alexander apartment,
small salon with
banqueting table

Page 42/43:
Stateroom of the Court
Library (now the National
Library)

a) Heldenplatz. Equestrian
statues by Anton Fernkorn:
Archduke Karl and Prince
Eugen of Savoy; at the
back, the Neue Burg
b) Monument to Prince
Eugen of Savoy: dome of
the Kunsthistorische
Museum
c) The outside of the
Burgtor, next to it the
Neue Burg, Corps de Logis

a) The Johann Strauss
memorial by Edmund
Hellmer (1923)
in the Stadtpark.
b) The "Wienflußportal"
in the Stadtpark
c) Minerva Fountain
outside the Austrian
Museum of Applied Arts,
Stubenring. Mosaic picture
by Antonio Salviati, 1873

c

a

b

c

Georg Coch-Platz: Otto
Wagner's Post Office
Savings Bank, main facade,
entrance area, side stairs

a

b

a) 3, Rennweg 2, Palais
Schwarzenberg, balustrade
with gambolling cherubs
b) A wing of the court of
honour
c) Statue of Field Marshal
Prince Schwarzenberg by
Ernst Julius Hähnel. To
the right, the former
palace of Archduke
Ludwig Viktor by
Heinrich Ferstel

b

a) Karlsplatz: Karlskirche
designed by Johann
Bernhard Fischer von
Erlach and his son, Joseph
Emanuel, Stadtbahn
pavilion by Otto Wagner
b) 1, Friedrichstrasse 12,
Secession, exhibition
premises by Josef Maria
Olbrich

a

b

a) Maria-Theresien-Platz
b, c) Statue of Empress
Maria Theresia by Kaspar
Zumbusch
b) Detail of the socle:
Chancellor Kaunitz,
General Laudon

a) Ornate stairway in the Burgtheater
b) View of the Burgtheater
c) Volksgarten

Page 60/61:
Parliament with the Athene Fountain by Karl Kundmann et al., completed 1902. Behind, the tower of the Town Hall

b

c

a) Town Hall, tower
passage, view of the
Votivkirche
b) Rear view of the
Votivkirche

Page 64/65:
Main facade of the Town
Hall

b

At the Schottentor: the
Creditanstalt and,
opposite, Theophil
Hansen's Palais Ephrussi,
University, Town Hall

Page 68/69:
Schottenring, Stock
Exchange

WHAT BECAME
OF THE
OLD SUBURBS

Soon after the building of the Leopoldine city wall in around 1200 small settlements grew up immediately outside the city gates. Protected only by abatis and by single towers, these defence "gaps" were burnt down on the approach of the Turks in 1529. Subsequently, a certain minimum space had to be observed when buildings were erected outside the city. The open zone, also known als the glacis, was extended on several occasions, finally to a distance of 600 paces in 1683. Originally it had been the site of hospitals, inns and trades considered undesirable in the town; as from mediaeval days noblemen and citizens also maintained gardens there. Later, numerous people unable to find lodgings in the city housed here. In times of war the inhabitants of the suburbs sought refuge within the walls. The second Turkish siege brought fresh destruction to all the suburbs, but these soon flourished again and within a few decades the city was surrounded by a garland of baroque garden palaces. In 1704 a fortification line was erected as a defence in case of raids by Hungarian rebels. It encompassed all the suburbs and enabled these to merge more quickly than hitherto. In 1850 the suburbs became a part of the municipality and comprised eight districts, the boundaries of which normally ran parallel to the main radial roads. Various regional peculiarities and social structures have nevertheless been retained until today in the suburbs. The fortifications remained quite significant until 1893, taxes being collected at their gates.

Landstrasse, the 3rd district, comprises the former suburbs of Landstrasse, Erdberg and Unter den Weissgerbern. The district boundary runs eastwards along the Danube Canal and follows the Prinz Eugen-Strasse and the Eastern Railway line in the west. The main axis of development was the Landstrasse, an old long distance route and a section of the Roman *limes.* Laid out between 1795 and 1805 and originally intended to connect Vienna with Trieste, the Wiener Neustadt Canal ended in a harbour basin outside the Stubentor; the bed of the abandoned canal was used in 1879 for the route of the railway line across the district. Urban development in this district commenced in the mid-19th century and is still underway. Even in this century large parts of this area were still used for cultivating vegetables.

Along the Landstrasse Hauptstrasse — originally the eastern exit route from the Roman camp — a suburb developed in the 12th century. Its centre is still distinguishable today. Until 1784 the Niklaskirche stood in the centre of this area, surrounded by a cemetery. Built in 1642, the Augustine monastery church of St. Rochus has been preserved and still defines the appearance of the road. The first section of the Hauptstrasse is dominated by the early 18th century convent. The remaining buildings are late 18th and early 19th century residential suburban houses of three to four storeys with long courtyard wings, interspersed with houses in the style of historicism and art nouveau. Between the Sechskrügelgasse and the Rochusgasse is a tiny square which was rebuilt in 1909 when it acquired its fountain. The Ungargasse probably dates back to Roman days and contains several houses going back to the period prior to the great building era in the late 19th century. Beethoven completed his Ninth Symphony in house no. 5 in 1824. Between the Ungargasse and the Wiener Neustadt Canal is the Veterinary University, a neo-Classical building which was erected between 1821 and 1823 according to plans by Johann Aman. In 1806 Prince Andreas Rasumovsky, the Russian ambassador, had his magnificent garden palace built by Louis Montoyer in large grounds to the east of the Landstrasse Hauptstrasse. The Geological Institute was housed here in 1851. Opposite the grammar school in the Kundmanngasse is the "Wittgenstein house" with its simple, cubic lines, designed in 1926 by Paul Engelmann, a pupil of Loos, in conjunction with Ludwig Wittgenstein, the philosopher. The farming settlement of Alt-Erdberg was originally mentioned in 1192. A commemorative tablet in the corridor of the house at Erdbergstrasse 41 is a reminder of King Richard the Lionheart being taken prisoner in 1192. Royal property for many years, the clustered village at Donauwagram already numbered 291 houses in 1779. Industry grew up along the banks of the Danube Canal in the second half of the 19th century, but by the end of that century Erdberg had become a slum and it was subsequently cleared. In its centre is the Parish Church of St. Peter and St. Paul — first mentioned in documents of 1353 — with a baroque, polychrome statue in front. Numerous council houses were built in the course of clearance and they include Robert Oerley's "Hanuschhof" (1924/25). The ground plan is of note, the facades having recesses which harbour the entrances. The "Rabenhof" by Schmidt and Aichinger was built at the same time. Providing an important link with the banks of the Danube, the Rabengasse forms the backbone of the site. One enters from the Hainburger Strasse through a monumental Gothic arched porch to reach the first courtyard, dominated by a tower-like block. Arcaded and Gothic arched openings characterize the site's appearance. The former Rennweger barracks took shape on the site of an orphanage, founded in 1742. The orphanage church was built in 1768 and at its consecration the twelve-year-old Mozart conducted his first mass, composed for the occasion. In 1797 the orphanage was converted into artillery barracks. Since then numerous changes have been made to the building. A riding arena was installed in the central courtyard in 1859/62 according to plans by August von Sicardsburg and Eduard van der Nüll. The old slaughterhouse was built in 1846/51, the central cattle market being added in 1880/83. The entrance in the Viehmarktgasse is notable for its two monumental sculptures of bulls by Anton Schmidgruber.

The quarter around the Arenbergpark was developed prior to the First World War in the grounds of the Palais Arenberg. It is a unique example of urban planning and architecture, comprising apartment houses with richly articulated facades dating back to the late 19th century. The apartment palaces surrounding the Dannebergplatz feature decorative facades with numerous balconies and oriels, the roof line frequently relieved by means of gables and attachments. Most of these buildings erected between 1906 and 1908 were designed by Georg Berger. Biedermeier and late 19th century houses alternate in the top section of the Ungargasse. The tone is set by the former Palais Sternberg, the last example of those garden palaces that once dominated here. As a contrast, the Portois & Fix store by Max Fabiani constitutes a milestone in modern Viennese architecture.

In its strategically favourable position on the high plateau in front of the Belvedere line, the arsenal is one of those impressive military buildings that were erected immediately after the 1848 Revolution. Serving both as barracks and as a centre of weapon manufacture, the artillery arsenal was designed by a group of notable architects: Eduard van der Nüll, August Sicard von Sicardsburg, Ludwig Förster, Theophil Hansen, Karl Rösner and Antonius Pius von Rigel. Completed between 1849 and 1855, the entire site comprised 72 buildings of compact appearance. The arsenal's artistic design was modelled on Italian fortresses during the Renaissance. Although major sections were destroyed during the War, it is still a compactly imposing 19th century citadel and one of the most outstanding examples of romantic historicism. A large section of the baroque garden

suburb has been preserved in the area between the Rennweg and the Prinz Eugen-Strasse on the gently rising slope of the arsenal terrace. Side by side at the foot of this slope are the Palais Schwarzenberg (1697/1728), the Untere Belvedere (1714/16) and the Salesian Convent (1679/99) by D. F. Allio and Fischer von Erlach the younger. The spacious gardens extend southwards, tapering to a point. Lukas von Hildebrandt's Belvedere Palace (1721) crowns the summit, one of Austrian baroque's most outstanding creations. The magnificent grounds are adjoined by the Botanical Gardens, commissioned by Maria Theresia in 1754 on the advice of Gerhard van Swieten, her personal physician. At the edge, its main facade facing the Jacquingasse, is the Convent of the Virgin of Three Miracles with its twin-spired neo-Romanesque church (1890/92). The front of the garden city on the Rennweg is formed by a sequence of impressive courtyarded buildings, culminating in the Salesian Convent and integrated domed church. The road opposite is characterized by the late baroque Guards' Church, the Palais Metternich (now the Italian Embassy) and the Convent of Sacre Coeur. In between are late 19th century apartment houses, among them three designed by Otto Wagner, who inhabited number 3 himself. North of the Rennweg between the Salesianergasse and the Rechter Bahngasse is the ambassadorial quarter. The Metternichgasse, Reisnerstrasse, Jaurèsgasse and Strohgasse are lined by representational residences, many of them with gardens. With its colourful onion domes, the Russian Orthodox Church provides a delightfully foreign touch amidst this elegance. When this quarter was enlarged, the older houses in the Salesianergasse and Marokkanergasse were replaced by new buildings, but there is still an entire row of Biedermeier houses in the Salesianergasse. Numerous imposing early 19th century buildings have been preserved

in the area between the Traungasse, Beatrixgasse and Heumarkt. With their representational neo-classical facades, the houses in Am Heumarkt 3 to 9 form part of the old "glacis front", so does the mint, built in 1838. The houses in Am Heumarkt 15 to 25 are of uniform appearance and were designed twenty years later according to plans by Anton Ölzelt.

The **Wieden** and **Margareten** districts were originally incorporated in the 4th district in 1850 and were not separated until 1861. They extend from the right bank of the river Wien across the flat northern slope of the Wienerberg. The 4th district comprises the suburbs of Wieden and Schaumburgergrund. This oldest and most important suburb developed along the long distance route south, its mediaeval centre being situated in the area of what today is the Rilkeplatz. Margareten comprises the suburb from which it acquired its name (after a chapel dedicated to St. Margaret of Antioch) plus Reinprechtsdorf, Laurenzergrund, Nikolsdorf, Hundsturm, Hungelbrunn and Matzleinsdorf. Once dominated by Favorita, the imperial country residence, and by other garden palaces, Wieden has always been a distinguished residential area, whereas Margareten was formed by local trade and has retained that character.

The Wiedner Hauptstrasse is a section of the old trunk road southwards. It features a characteristic sequence of little triangles at junctions and forks. Urban building commenced here in the 18th century, but few of the late 18th century or Biedermeier houses have been preserved in their original state. Most were rebuilt or replaced. Various different building stages can be distinguished in the Wiedner Hauptstrasse. The first section is much changed due to the rebuilding of the site of the old Starhemberg house. The triangle at the fork of the Favoritenstrasse is dominated by the early baroque facade of the Paulanerkirche. Christoph Willibald Gluck spent the last years of his life in the house at Wiedner Hauptstrasse 32, dying here on 15th November, 1787. The triangle at the intersection of the Schaumburgergasse is adorned by Anton Paul Wagner's fountain (1893). Once lined by four rows of trees, the Mayerhofgasse leads to the central projecting bay of the Theresianum; the south side consists of late Biedermeier houses. The following section of the Wiedner Hauptstrasse culminates in the square formed by the avenue in front of the Church of St. Thekla and the adjoining Piarist monastery and school. The Palais Schönburg-Hartenstein on the Rainergasse is one of the last remnants of the baroque garden suburb and was built in 1705 for Count Thomas Gundacker Starhemberg, probably by J. L. Hildebrandt. The entrance to the garden — once larger and of baroque design — is flanked by mighty sphinxes.

The Prinz Eugen-Strasse, formerly the Heugasse, developed in the 17th century as a local route and now constitutes one of the main access roads to the southern districts of the city. At the end of the 19th century magnificent palaces and residential houses were built in the immediate vicinity of the Belvedere Palace and they still give this road its character. The focal point of the steeply rising Argentinierstrasse is the neo-Gothic Church of St. Elizabeth (1860/66), set in a tree-lined square.

The lower section of the Favoritenstrasse is dominated by the elongated main facade of the Theresianum. Comprising several courtyards, the huge complex dates back to 'Favorita', the imperial summer residence that was first built in 1616/25, then rebuilt by Ludovico Burnacini after destruction in the 1683 siege of Vienna by the Turks. It was later extended on several occasions. This garden palace marks the beginning of the garden suburb. The Mozartplatz was laid out and built up in 1798; its southern side still contains the four-storey apartment houses with little

front gardens, built at that time. The Magic Flute Fountain (1905) is by Carl Wollek and Otto Schönthal. The Brahmsplatz further south was laid out at the turn of the century, five-storey apartment houses being grouped around a tiny park.

The buildings in the quarter between the Heumühlgasse, Margaretenstrasse and Pilgramgasse, once a part of the Wieden suburb, date back mainly to the Biedermeier period and the late 19th century. Several Biedermeier houses have been preserved in the lower section of the Heumühlgasse. In the Kettenbrückengasse and the Franzensstrasse, both laid out in 1827, most of the original buildings still exist in compact groups. Franz Schubert died in the house at Kettenbrückengasse 6 (formerly Lumpertgasse 694) on 19th November, 1828. Branching off the Margaretenstrasse, the Freundgasse still retains the appearance of a late baroque suburban street with its three-storey houses and their little courtyards. The centre of the district is the Margaretenplatz which was laid out in around 1725 in front of the palace of the same name. The latter was built in the 16th century and sections of it have been preserved, although they are changed beyond recognition. A more significant example of urban planning is the Margaretenhof, built in 1884 on the site of the old brewery according to plans by Ferdinand Fellner and Hermann Helmer. Intended to replace the palace as the focal point of the district, the building complex — a row of houses in a private road with front gardens — is a remarkable creation according to the principles of late Viennese historicism.

In the years following the First World War council houses were built along the Margartengürtel. The first such building was the Metzleinstalerhof by Robert Kalesa and Hubert Gessner. In 1924 the neighbouring Reumannhof was added. Planned by Gessner, a pupil of Otto Wagner's, it is one of the most outstanding examples of the

architecture and urban planning of social housing between the Wars. The monumental site, symmetrically grouped around a central courtyard, is screened from the road by covered ways and pavilions. The Matteotihof, Herwegh-Hof and Julius Popp-Hof were built in the following years by Heinrich Schmidt and Hermann Aichinger. This imposing series of buildings was rounded off in 1928 by the Franz Domes-Hof, Margaretengürtel 126—134, planned by Peter Behrens, the notable German architect.

Mariahilf, the 6th district, was created by uniting the suburbs of Mariahilf, Gumpendorf, Laimgrube, Magdalenengrund und Windmühle. It comprises the southern section of the Schmelzterrasse descending to the river Wien; the northern boundary is formed by the Mariahilfer Strasse, which runs along the ridge. The name "Laimgrube" is a reference to the clay pits which were a feature of this area in the Middle Ages. Mariahilf was originally called Im Schöff, its later name (Mariahilf = Our Lady of Succour) referring to a miraculous image erected in a cemetery chapel in around 1670, later the site of the church of the same name. The small borough of Magdalenengrund originally belonged to the benefice of the Magdalene Chapel (1338) at St. Stephen's. In the Middle Ages wine growing was the chief occupation in the district, but later numerous artisans settled here. After the second Turkish siege garden palaces were built in this area and by the 19th century it had acquired a dense network of roads and buildings. The majority of the houses built at that time have been replaced once and even twice.

Forming the boundary between the 6th and 7th district, the Mariahilfer Strasse is an ancient route. Built up as far as the Gürtel in the 18th century, it became one of Vienna's main shopping streets in the late 19th century and consequently changed its appearance on several occasions. House no. 45 "Zum goldenen Hirschen" is an important reminder of the old buildings: as the birthplace of Ferdinand Raimund, the Austrian author, it holds historic significance. The house at no. 55 and the adjoining Barnabite monastery both date back to the late baroque era. The square surrounding the Parish and Pilgrimage Church of the Ascension of the Virgin is the old centre of Mariahilf. The church and the Barnabitengasse, with its old trees and its strainer arch, present a picturesque scene that is enhanced still further by the oversized late 17th century crucifixion group. The top section of the Windmühlgasse is dominated by the Church of St. Joseph ob der Laimgrube. Originally this stood in the Mariahilfer Strasse, but it was moved here in 1906 for traffic reasons. The junction of the Schadekgasse, Barnabitengasse, Windmühlgasse and Kaunitzgasse forms an unusual arrangement which is marked by a steep descent. The entire area is dominated by the flak tower in the Esterhazypark. The corner house at Kaunitzgasse-Gumpendorfer Strasse was built as a theatre in 1904 and converted into a cinema in 1929.

The area that descends steeply from the Mariahilfer Strasse to the river Wien is marked by the terrain. The great differences in level — the result of centuries of clay pit workings — are partially overcome by steps, these including the remarkable Fillgraderstiege (1905—1907). The Millöckergasse-Papagenogasse area is defined by late 18th century buildings, its centre is the Theater an der Wien, built between 1779 and 1801 and later altered on several occasions. The delightful Papagenotor provides the highlight in the street of the same name. At the junction of the Girardigasse, Lehargasse and Gumpendorfer Strasse is a late 19th century corner building containing a typical Viennese cafe with its original decor; adjoining it to the east is the former court theatre repository by Semper

and Hasenauer (1880). In the Linke Wienzeile — rebuilt after 1880 with representational apartment houses — the artistic highlights are provided by Otto Wagner's houses at 38 and 40, the corner house with gilded stucco ornamentation to a design by Kolo Moser and the colourful splendour of the majolica house.

Gumpendorf was first mentioned in 1135/40. The original centre in the area of the Brückengasse-Gumpendorfer Strasse displays the characteristics of a clustered village. The Ägydiuskirche was built in 1765/70, whereas the houses framing the church square date back to different periods of the 19th century and form a group of suburban appearance. The Sandwirtgasse was built up after 1852, many of the original houses have been preserved. Number 18 housed the studio used jointly by Gustav Klimt and Franz Matsch. The western row of the Haydngasse forms a remarkable suburban complex: the two-storey house at no. 29 dates back to 1793 and belonged to Joseph Haydn. He died here on 31st May, 1809. Today it contains the Municipality of Vienna's Haydn Museum.

Neubau, the 7th district, was formed by merging the suburbs of Neubau, Spittelberg and Schottenfeld and parts of Laimgrube, Mariahilf, St. Ulrich and Altlerchenfeld. Like most of the inner districts, it extends from the old glacis boundary to the defence line, that is from the Lastenstrasse to the Gürtel in today's terms. It is bounded by the Mariahilfer Strasse in the south and the Lerchenfelder Strasse in the north. The oldest of the suburbs was Zeismannsbrunn which was later named after the Parish Church of St. Ulrich, consecrated in 1211. In 1693 a newer, westerly part of the suburb was divided off; originally called Neustift, it acquired the name Neubau and this passed to the district. The borough of Spittelberg dates back to the same period. The buildings in the area west of the Neubaugasse are younger. This

area has borne the name Schottenfeld since 1777 and was a manufacturing quarter. In fact, the entire district is still characterized by trade and commerce.

The eastern section of the area between the Mariahilfer Strasse and the Siebensterngasse is dominated by the extensive complex of the Stiftskaserne barracks. The main front of the barracks is situated in the Stiftgasse and the portals are decorated with armorial bearings. The wing of the barracks in the Mariahilfer Strasse was entirely rebuilt between 1873 and 1875. In the west of this area, the Mondscheingasse takes an oddly winding course, following the boundary of the old St. Ulrich cemetery. The first section of the Neubaugasse contains remarkable residential and office buildings dating back to the turn of the century. A delightful contrast is provided by the remaining Biedermeier house at no. 16. The lower section of the Neustiftgasse is dominated by the side of the Palais Trautson and the rusticated facade of the Mechitarist Church, its present appearance dating back to the conversion in 1871 by Camillo Sitte. Next to it is Kornhäusel's monastery (1835). The row of houses opposite in the Mechitaristengasse go back to the Biedermeier era. There is a charming passageway with heightened arcades and delightful glimpses, running from no. 16 in the Neustiftgasse to no. 13 in the Lerchenfelder Strasse.

The square-like arrangement at the junction of the Kellermanngasse is accentuated by the Augustine fountain of 1908. Some of the older buildings here date back to the 16th century. The elevated situation of the late baroque Parish Church of St. Ulrich — wide steps lead up to the porch — is a reminder that long ago, before it was properly contained, the Ottakringer stream used to reach a dangerous level.

Access to the Spittelberg quarter between the Burggasse, Siebensterngasse, Breitegasse and Stiftgasse is afforded by four parallel streets. The area comprises five narrow blocks of buildings with small plots of land. The little suburb was founded in 1675 and, after the few houses were destroyed in the Turkish siege, it was resettled, the hospital being the new landlord — hence the name "Spittelberg". The majority of the two to three-storey baroque buildings with little inner courtyards have been preserved. The atmosphere of old Viennese suburban streets can be sensed here.

Laid out in the mid-18th century, the Schottenfeld was a silk-weaving centre in the manufacturing age. In around 1800 the factories here employed many workers. The area was popularly know as "Brillantengrund" (Diamond Land) on account of the proverbial wealth of the factory owners. Street names like Seidengasse (Silk Street) or Bandgasse (Ribbon Street) are a reminder of those days. Production sites still exist today in this area. The Church of St. Laurence (1786) and the priest's house on the highest point of the terrain are the only remaining original buildings. The last section of the Lerchenfelder Strasse is dominated by the most outstanding example of the romantic revival — Altlerchenfeld Parish Church "of the Seven Refuges" which was commenced in 1848 according to plans by Paul Sprenger and completed by Eduard van der Nüll according to altered designs by Johann Georg Müller. With its octagonal crossing tower and its mighty roof, the Lazarist Church of the Conception in the Kaiserstrasse still commands the scene. A neo-Gothic brick building, it was designed in 1860/62 by Friedrich von Schmidt, the first of his Viennese works. The square in front is flanked by 20th century buildings and is screened from the road by high railings.

Josefstadt, the 8th district, comprises the former suburbs of Josefstadt, Strozzigrund and Breitenfeld, as well as parts of St. Ulrich, Lerchenfeld and

Alservorstadt. The district boundaries of 1850 were shifted from the Floriani-gasse to the Alser Strasse in 1862. The wide ridge between Ottakringerbach and Alserbach was not settled until late. Most of the areas in agricultural use were the property of the "Schottenstift". The elongated Ler-chenfelder Strasse, Josefstädter Strasse, Florianigasse and Alser Strasse were originally old routes between the fields. After the second Turkish siege the Josefstadt developed on the "Buchfeld" fields upon the instructions of the Marchese Hyppolith Malaspina. The representational square in front of the Church of "Maria Treu" formed the centre of the new suburb. The Lerchenfeld was settled at the same time, the Strozzi garden palace being built here in 1702. Soon, other splendid summer residences were built in the Alservorstadt. The area by the fortification line, still open land, was designated building land in 1801 by Benno Pointner, abbot of the "Schottenstift". An orthogonal road network developed, its two squares (Bennoplatz and Albertplatz) being typical of the early 19th century. Unlike Mariahilf and Neubau, the eighth district was predominantly a residential area. Gradually, the marked social differences disappeared between the artisan suburbs of Altlerchenfeld and Strozzi-grund, the bourgeois Josefstadt and the more grand Alservorstadt. South of the Josefstädter Strasse there is a notable little building complex sited on garden plots which were once a part of the Palais Strozzi. This baroque palace still exists, but was hidden from view by a new wing, built in 1878. The Lange Gasse and Neudeggergasse feature baroque and Biedermeier houses amongst late 19th century buildings. The southern section of the Trautsongasse is taken up by the garden wall and orangery of the Palais Auersperg, in the northern section the Beethoven house at no. 2 is worthy of note. The street is accentuated by a strainer arch between

the palace and house no. 4. Of the spacious baroque buildings between the Alser Strasse and the Florianigasse only the Minorite (once Trinitarian) monastery still exists, together with the Church of the Holy Trinity (1727) and the former Schönborn summer palace, now the Museum of Folklore. Its grounds have been open to the public since 1862. In the top section of the Laudongasse two typical mid-19th century apartment blocks have been preserved — the Mölkerhof and the Bernardhof. Rudolf von Alt, the painter, lived and died in the neighbouring Kleiner Bernardhof. The Wiener Stadttheater was built in the square opposite in 1913, but disappeared in 1961.

One of the most outstanding building complexes in the Josefstadt is the Biedermeier ensemble between Landesgerichtsstrasse and Buchfeldgasse; it has been preserved almost in its entirety. Notable 18th century buildings adorn the Lenaugasse, the row of houses on the city side dates back to around 1840, however. On the edge of the Josefstadt the former Institute of Military Geography provides an architectonic focal point; it was built in 1842 and a further storey was added in 1871. The elongated front of Paul Sprenger's Provincial Court building also formed part of the representational glacis facade of the Josefstadt and Alsergrund suburbs. The historic heart of the Josefstadt is to be found in the area between Langegasse—Josefstädter Strasse—Lederergasse-Florianigasse; the remarkable baroque square in front of the Church of "Maria Treu" is flanked by the Piarist College and the former Löwenburg Seminary. Based on a 1698 design by Hildebrandt and later altered on several occasions, the church acquired its magnificent ceiling frescos in 1752, these being the work of Maulbertsch. The central section of the Langegasse contains late baroque and Biedermeier groups and apartment houses dating back to the late 19th century and the

76

art nouveau period. The Josefstädter Strasse also features remains of earlier buildings, among them the Josefstädter Theater, which was opened in 1788 and rebuilt on several occasions.

Alsergrund, the 9th district, comprises the former suburbs of Althan, Himmelpfortgrund, Liechtenthal, Michelbeuern, Rossau, Thury and the greater part of Alservorstadt; it consists of a strip of alluvial land beside the Danube Canal and a terrace landscape interspersed by the Alserbach and Währingerbach streams. The Liechtensteinstrasse once followed the original bank of the Danube, whereas the first section of the Währinger Strasse and the Nussdorfer Strasse correspond to the Roman *limes* road to Klosterneuburg; the Alser Strasse follows the Roman route through the Vienna Woods to the Tullnerfeld. The borough of Michelbeuern developed in the late 18th century on land which had been the property of the Salzburg Benedictine Abbey of Michaelbeuern since around 1170. The Himmelpfortgrund on the Nussdorfer Strasse bears the name of a Viennese convent of nuns, landowners there since 1639. Adjoining this to the south, between the Nussdorfer Strasse and the Alserbachstrasse, the suburb of Himmelpfortgrund was founded in 1646 by Johann Thury, a court servant and brickyard owner. Liechtenthal, the neighbouring day-labourers' suburb, was laid out between 1705 and 1712 by Prince Johann Adam Liechtenstein. In subsequent years Liechtenthal Parish Church of the 14 Holy Helpers was built. Franz Schubert, who was born in the district on 31st January, 1797, was christened in this church. The last remains of old Liechtenthal only disappeared recently. The Rossau suburb developed from a fishing village in the flood-endangered wetland area known as the "Oberer Werd" in mediaeval days. All that remains of the tiny hamlet of Althan — in the 18th century it was the manorial seat of the family of the

same name — is the block of houses formed by the Fechtergasse, Simon Denk-Gasse and Alserbachstrasse. A large part of the Alservorstadt also belongs to the district; situated on both sides of the Alserbach, it developed in the mid-17th century. When these suburbs were incorporated in the municipality, marked architectural and social differences still existed. By the turn of the century these had largely been absorbed in the melting-pot of the big city, but some reminders still exist on the edges of the area.

The Alser Strasse is the site of the huge Old General Hospital which developed from the poor-house founded in 1963. After being extended and redesigned in the 18th and 19th century, the complex now comprises nine buildings, grouped around an avenue. The "Narrenturm", a mad-house built by Isidor Canevale in 1784, features an unusual circular ground-plan. Adjoining it to the east is the former Garrison Hospital. The hospital district is impressively concluded by the Josephinum (1785), the former surgical-medical Military Academy. The Technological Trade Museum was built in 1875 as the administrative centre of a locomotive factory. The Otto Wagner-Platz adjoining the hospital is dominated by the monumental edifice of the National Bank, built between 1918 and 1925. The blocks of apartment houses approaching the Votivkirche date back to the decades around the turn of the century. Designed by Otto Wagner, the house at Garnisongasse 1 is a true focal point with its unusual facade. The land between the General Hospital and the Währinger Strasse was first built up when a monastery there was dissolved. The little houses in the Van Swieten-Gasse date back to the 18th century.

The monastery garden was built up after 1840, the Lackierergasse and the Beethovengasse and their late Biedermeier houses taking shape then. The last building to be built in this area

was the "Schwarzspanierhof" (1904) which took the place of the house where Beethoven died.

East of the Währinger Strasse the terrain falls sharply to the bank of the Danube. The Servite monastery in the Rossau suburb started to take shape in 1639. Completed in 1677, the church and its ornate interior survived the Turkish siege. The Liechtenstein summer palace was built between 1691 and 1711 according to plans by Domenico Martinelli. Originally, the site of Heinrich Ferstel's "widow's palace" (1875) in the north of the garden was taken up by Johann Bernhard Fischer von Erlach's small belvedere. Another remnant of the garden suburb of yore is the Dietrichstein Park with Heinrich Koch's neo-classical palace (1834). This area features another monumental building — Anton Ospel's Spanish Hospital at Boltzmanngasse 7—9 and the Church of Maria de Mercede, now the archiepiscopal priests' seminary.

In 1852 the military exchequer started to dispose of the glacis land south of the Berggasse in order to finance Rossau barracks. The residential quarter that developed here betwen 1852 and 1860 was called "New Vienna". Most of the buildings have been preserved in their original state and are regarded as the forerunners of the apartment blocks on the Ringstrasse. In the sixties, the area to the east of the Wasagasse was developed. Built in 1865, the Harmonietheater and the housing complex in the Harmoniegasse were designed by the young Otto Wagner. The area surrounding the Strudlhof — this was demolished in around 1800 and was the site of the oldest Viennese Academy of Art in 1700 — became an exclusive residential district at the end of the 19th century. The Strudlhofstiege, a flight of steps leading to the tree-lined Strudlhofgasse, was immortalized in a novel by Heimito von Doderer.

Building work on the right bank of the Danube Canal, the boundary of the 9th district, started in around 1875. The long front of decorative facades on the Rossauer Lände is concluded by Emil Förster's police building, which was completed in 1904. To the south of this stands the impressive, fortress-like Rossauer barracks, visible from afar in a commanding position.

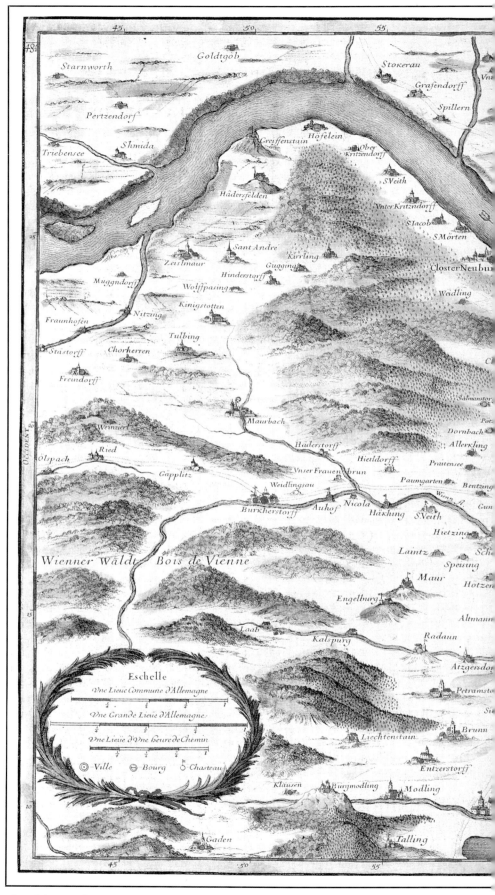

Plan of the city of Vienna and surroundings, 1695

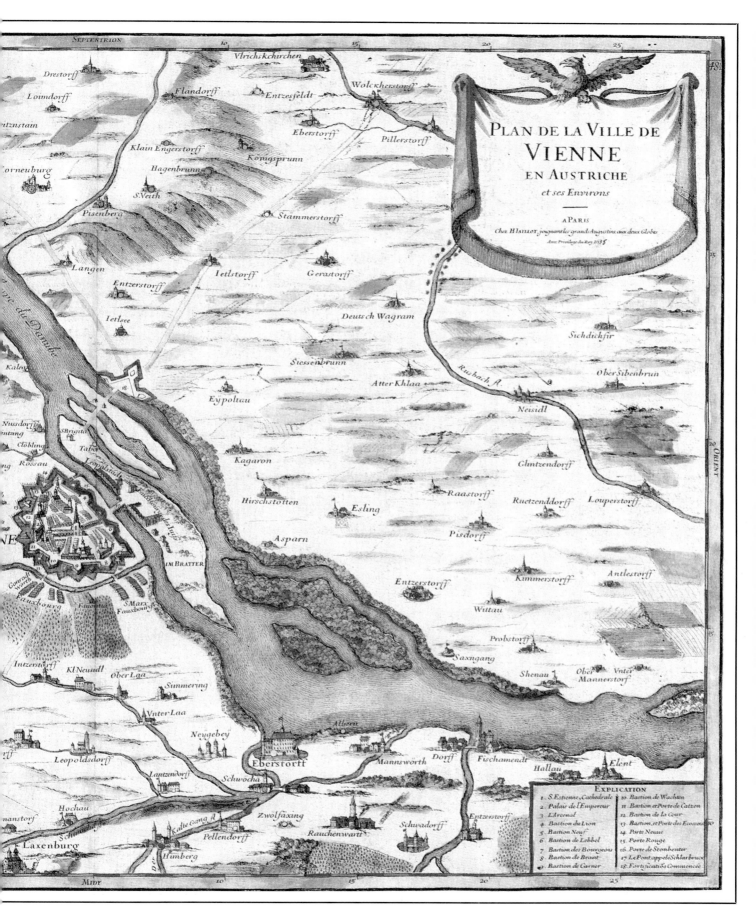

PLAN DE LA VILLE DE
VIENNE
EN AUSTRICHE
et ses Environs

A PARIS
Chez H JAILLOT, joignant les grands Augustins aux deux Globes
Avec Privilege du Roy 1685

EXPLICATION

1. S. Estienne, Cathedrale	10. Bastion de Wachten
2. Palais de l'Empereur	11. Bastion et Porte de Catzen
3. L'Arcenal	12. Bastion de la Cour
4. Bastion du Lion	13. Bastion, et Porte des Ecossois
5. Bastion Neuf	14. Porte Neuue
6. Bastion de Lebbel	15. Porte Rouge
7. Bastion des Bourgeois	16. Porte de Stonbenter
8. Bastion de Brant	17. Le Pont appelé Schlarbruck
9. Bastion de Carner	18. Fortificatiõs Cõmencée

79

a

b

The Lower Belvedere and
the Upper Belvedere
were erected in 1714 to
1716 and 1721 to 1723
respectively by Johann
Lukas von Hildebrandt
for Prince Eugene of
Savoy.
a) Sphinxes and
horse-breaker in
front of the palace.
b) View from the Upper
to the Lower Belvedere
and across the rooftops of
Vienna with St. Stephen's
Cathedral.
c) South facade of
the Upper Belvedere.

Page 84—86:
6, Linke Wienzeile 38,
Köstlergasse 1, apartment
house by Otto Wagner

Page 87:
6, Linke Wienzeile 40,
apartment house by Otto
Wagner, so-called
"majolica house"

a, b) Spittelberg
c, d) 7, Mentergasse 13,
Altlerchenfeld vicarage

Page 88/89:
Flea market held on
Saturdays at the Nasch-
markt

c

d

b

c

a) 8, Josefstädter Strasse 26, Entrance to the Theater in der Josefstadt

Page 92/93:
a) 9, Währinger Strasse 25, Josephinum, Hygeia Fountain by Johann Martin Fischer
b) Mariahilfer Strasse
c) 4, Favoritenstrasse 15, Theresianum

b

THE DONAUINSEL

Before it was built up, the Danube was a raging torrent, its wetlands interspersed with numerous branches, islands and sandbanks. When it was incorporated in the municipality in 1850, **Leopoldstadt,** the 2nd district, comprised the entire island formed by the Danube Canal and what today is the Old Danube, i. e. the suburb of Leopoldstadt, Brigittenau — this was not partitioned off until 1900 — and Kaisermühlen, which became a part of the new 22nd district in 1938. This area was first settled, albeit sparsely, in the Middle Ages, the Taborstrasse being the only exit route to the north until the Danube was built up. The Augarten and Prater, both royal hunting grounds, played a decisive part in this development. They still comprise large open areas and are two of Vienna's major recreation sites. The Praterstrasse took shape in around 1570 as the access route to the royal hunting grounds. After the Prater was opened to the general public in 1766, the suburb rapidly developed. At one time the Prater-strasse was regarded as one of the grandest suburban streets, becoming the main northern exit route after the construction of the Reichsbrücke (originally called the Kronprinz-Rudolf-Brücke) in 1876.

The characteristic view of St. Stephen's Church was probably an intentional feature when this area was laid out; it acquired emphasis by "perspectively" narrowing the alignment of the houses. Frequently branching off at an acute angle, the side streets are also unusual; the houses at the crossroads were frequently accentuated architectonically. The present buildings date back to various periods. The Palais Bellegarde, the "Zum grünen Jäger" inn, various imposing houses and Karl Rösner's Church of St. John of Nepomuk (1841/46) have been preserved, the latter providing emphasis in the central section of the Praterstrasse. An apartment house in the style of a quattrocento Venetian palazzo, the Dogenhof is remarkable. On the bank of the Danube, adjoining the approach to the Reichsbrücke, the Imperial Jubilee Church (now the Church of Francis of Assisi) was built between 1898 and 1913 in neo-romantic style according to plans by Viktor Luntz.

The Augarten was originally royal hunting terrain and a hunting lodge was said to have been built here in 1614 for Emperor Matthias. In 1677 Leopold I merged various properties into extensive pleasure grounds. Taken over by the court, the Trautson garden palace was destroyed in 1683 and not rebuilt. The existing Augarten palace was created from a manor house belonging to Zacharias Leeb, a councillor; last rebuilt in 1896, it has housed the Vienna Boys' Choir since 1948. The Viennese Porcelain Factory occupies the building originally built in 1705 for Eleonore, the Queen Mother. Joseph I had the Obere Augartenstrasse laid out to improve access. In 1712 the extensive gardens were redesigned by Jean Trehet, the famous French landscape gardener; most of the avenues and shrubberies date back to that period. Joseph II had the garden porch built by Isidor Canevale in 1775. The Obere Augartenstrasse is lined with 18th and 19th century buildings that once served as accommodation for court servants. In the row opposite the park the Palais Grassalkovics (1780) is particularly remarkable.

The area between the Taborstrasse, Kleine Pfarrgasse, Leopoldsgasse and Tandelmarktgasse forms the old centre of the Leopoldstadt. A treeless heath, it was made over to the Jewish community in 1625 and after their eviction it was taken over by the municipality of Vienna in 1669. A few 17th century houses (Haidgasse 6, 8 and 9, Grosse Sperlgasse 16, 18, 20 and 24) dating back to the period prior to the second Turkish siege still remain, rare examples of suburban buildings of that period. Built in 1670 in place of the synagogue and later enlarged, the Church of St. Leopold and the neighbouring house (1736)

The Augarten bridge, Laurenz Janscha, 1792

In the Prater, near the coffee-houses, Jakob Alt, 1824

are the oldest buildings in the Grosse Pfarrgasse. The tone of the lower section of the Taborstrasse is set by the Commodity Exchange, built by Carl König in 1890 and crowned by a powerful attic storey, decorated with figures. The remaining baroque buildings include the monastery and hospital of the monks hospitaller, founded in 1614. The Karmeliterplatz and the monastery church of St. Joseph (completed in 1669) effect the transition to a "Josephine" quarter in the area that developed on the grounds of the Carmelite monastery that was dissolved in 1783.

The Prater is mentioned in a document of Emperor Friedrich Barbarossa's, dated 2nd July, 1162. King Ferdinand I had a cutting, the Hauptallee, made through the swamps here in 1537 as the quickest means of reaching Simmering. His successor, Maximilian II, closed the Prater to the public in order to establish hunting grounds there. For centuries the district remained out of bounds to the population until Joseph II again

opened the Prater to the general public in 1766. The newly designed Praterstern and the Tegetthof column built in 1886 became the real centre of the district. The "Wurstelprater", a popular amusement site, has undergone many changes in the course of the years. Amidst the fairground magic the giant wheel towers up; constructed by an English company in 1897, it is one of Vienna's most familiar landmarks. The "Nobelprater" stretches along the 4.5 km. Hauptallee to Isidor Canevale's summer house (1782), a neo-classical building. Since time immemorial the Prater has been the site of sporting events. In 1878 the trotting racecourse in the Krieau was opened. Since then numerous other sports sites have been constructed. Completed in 1931 and enlarged on several occasions since, the stadium attracts huge crowds. Before the Danube Canal was built in 1832, the Freudenau — said to have been the site of tournaments and other contests in the Middle Ages — was part of Simmering Heath, the

racecourse being installed after the foundation of the Jockey Club in 1862. Several stands were erected in 1872 according to plans by Carl von Hasenauer. The major part of the existing building dates back to 1885/87 and was designed by Anton and Josef Drexler. With its beautiful trees, this racecourse is among the loveliest in Europe.

Brigittenau, the 20th district, extends as far as the Augarten. The area was originally called Schottenau or Wolfsau, the name Brigittenau — so the legend goes — being connected with a chapel of that name, built in the 17th century during the Thirty Years War. The Taborstrasse of today, a major route to the bridges over the Danube, ran through the middle of this hunting ground and grazing land which was not settled until the 18th century. During Joseph II's reign the Brigittenau became a popular site for excursions. After the course of the river Danube was regulated in 1875, building work started. Within a few decades a densely populated residential and industrial district had developed, crossed by numerous roads. In the Meldemannstrasse there is a building of particular note — a lodging house for men, designed by Leopold Ramsauer and Otto Richter on the model of the Rowton houses in London. The Winarsky-Hof, a block of flats built by the Council in 1924, was a co-production by famous architects like Peter Behrens, Josef Frank, Josef Hoffmann, Oskar Strnad and Oskar Wlach. A rectangular building set around a central quadrangle is enclosed by a loose square of houses. The Leystrasse crosses the site, the perspective of which is accentuated by the arrangement of the four imposing gateways. The impressive council block on Friedrich Engels-Platz was designed (1930 to 1933) by Rudolf Perco, a pupil of Otto Wagner's. The facade on view from Engels-Platz is conceived in the manner of a triumphal portal.

Augarten:
the garden entrance,
built by Isidor Canevale
in 1775.

Page 101:
The Palais Augarten
is the home of the
Vienna Boys' Choir

101

a) Wurstelprater and giant
wheel
b) Prater: stands on
Freudenau racecourse
c) The main avenue in late
autumn

Tegetthoff monument at the Praterstern by Karl von Hasenauer and Karl Kundmann

AROUND
THE WIENERBERG

Until the mid-19th century the only buildings in **Favoriten,** now the 10th district, were in the villages of Oberlaa and Unterlaa on the periphery. Urban settlement did not develop until after the construction of the Southern and Eastern Railways (1841 and 1846) and followed the Favoriten and Laxenburger Strasse. Built by speculators, the cheap blocks of flats were first let to railway workers and labourers employed in building the arsenal nearby. At the time of the stock exchange crash in 1873 — this put an end to construction work for the time being — there were 25,800 inhabitants. Administered by the Wieden district at that time, the area forms the centre of the 10th district, which was established in 1874. The first district outside the fortification line, it acquired its name from Favorita, the former imperial country seat, later the Theresianum. It comprises the Wienerberg and Laaerberg and is bounded by the railway lines to the north and the east. Until recently, large areas here were used by brick-yards. Between the Wars numerous large council buildings took shape in Favoriten and it was here that the first big estates were built after the Second World War.

On the summit of the Wienerberg, next to the "Spinnerin am Kreuz" column — this was erected in 1379 and rebuilt on several occasions — several blocks of council flats were built, as well as a large site owned by the Municipal Waterworks. Visible from afar, the water-tower has in a way acquired the function of the old Gothic wayside column as a milestone at the apex of the hill. The George Washington-Hof was erected between 1927 and 1930 according to plans by Karl Krist and Robert Oerley. The buildings differ in their architectonic arrangement and in the plants from which their names are derived. The dominant elements in the Birkenhof (birch) and the Fliederhof (lilac) are large semi-circular window openings, whereas the Ulmenhof (elm) is

characterized by steep gables and pebbledash rendering decorated with rhomboid ornaments. The site was named after Georg Washington in 1932 on the occasion of the 200th birthday of the first American President. The Am Wasserturm garden estate was designed in 1925 by Franz Schuster and Franz Schacherl and consists of simply arranged cubic buildings, in pairs or terraced, generally two-storeyed, with hipped roofs. A picturesque, co-ordinated entity was aimed at when the site was laid out. The bread factory founded by Heinrich and Fritz Mendel in 1891 was constructed in several phases and is an interesting example of early 20th century industrial architecture. Crowned by a high pyramidal roof, the huge silo at the end of the factory front in the Absberggasse is significant from an urban planning point of view. The so-called labourers' cottage site in the immediate vicinity was built for labourers and artisans at the Anker bread factory in 1896 by the Emperor Francis Joseph Jubilee Foundation for Social Housing and Welfare Amenities according to plans by Josef Unger. It consists of eighteen two-storey houses for single families, arranged in groups of three to six houses. The various groups are of uniform appearance. The ground floors are in rough brickwork, the upper floors featuring plastering arrangements. The eaves and gables are decorated with turned, open-work, chamfered wood. The skilfully arranged gardens are a characteristic feature of the site. The idea of workers' cottages was introduced from England in the mid-19th century. There were numerous examples in the days of the monarchy, but few have been preserved.

Oberlaa and Unterlaa were first mentioned as "Lo" at the end of the 12th century. Today's village settlements along the road probably developed on the banks of the Liesingbach. The main influence is still agriculture and the buildings frequently have gables

on the front facing the road. Oberlaaer Platz is dominated by the late baroque Parish Church, the old rectory opposite and the baroque, gabled house adjoining it to the east. Amongst the various rural buildings in Unterlaa the 18th century Prentlhof is outstanding with its interior fresco decorations, so is the mill on the Liesing, its archway bearing the date 1777.

Set between the Danube Canal and the Eastern Railway, **Simmering,** the 11th district, comprises the place of that name, the old rural settlement of Kaiser-Ebersdorf and parts of Schwechat and Kledering; it is cut through by the Simmeringer Hauptstrasse, an arterial road that has existed since Roman days. Urban development on a large scale did not commence until around 1880. Large areas of the district are still open ground, market gardens alternating with industrial land. Simmering gasworks (1896/99) on the right bank of the Danube Canal is a remarkable example of late 19th century industrial architecture. The gasometers can be seen from afar and provide the main accent. Their architectonic arrangement is reminiscent of the shapes encountered in early Italian buildings. The first municipal electricity works were installed here not long afterwards. The heart of old Simmering lies at the fork of Simmeringer Hauptstrasse and Kaiser-Ebersdorfer Strasse. Set on a hill above the ancient *limes,* the place was first mentioned in 1028 as Simanningen, but it is probably much older. Leading up to the baroque facade of the old Church of St. Laurence, the Kobelgasse has retained the character of a village centre. Here is the little Biedermeier schoolhouse, opposite it a village house and next to it the rectory with its delightful art nouveau facade. The little old cemetery surrounding the church is an integral part of the village scene.

In 1784 a communal cemetery was laid out in front of the St. Marx

View of Vienna from the "Spinnerin am Kreuz"

ramparts and burials took place here until 1874. The design of the tombstones is predominantly classicist and Biedermeier. St. Marx Cemetery enjoys world renown on account of the fact that Wolfgang Amadeus Mozart was buried here on 6th December, 1791. The picturesque grounds were re-opened to the public in 1937. The decision to build a Central Cemetery was taken by the Council in 1886, the design being entrusted to Alfred Friedrich Bluntschli of Zurich and Karl Jonas Mylius of Frankfurt am Main. It was opened in 1874. The representational buildings near the main entrance were erected in 1905 according to plans by

Max Hegele, a pupil of Otto Wagner's. The severely symmetric gateway consists of two cubic administrative wings and two obelisk-shaped pylons. Culminating in semi-circular arcades with vaults in the south, the entrance is flanked by the mortuaries. The main axis leads through the graves of honour to the circular site of the presidents' vault. Behind this is the cemetery church (1907/10), named after Karl Lueger, the mayor of Vienna, who is buried here. To the left and right of the church are architrave vaults, domed at the corners, over a quadrantal groundplan. The monumental site is characteristic of the pompous late 19th

century grave cult. In 1922 the crematorium by Clemens Holzmeister was built in the gardens of the Neugebäude opposite the Central Cemetery; it is a remarkable example of "expressionist" architecture. The Neugebäude was built during Maximilian II's reign in the imperial hunting grounds, but it was never completed and in 1775 it passed to the military authority for use as a powder-magazine. A large part of the site has been preserved, although its appearance has been altered. The main building, once open on all sides, is completely walled-in, so are the stables and the menageries building. The outer enclosing wall is more or less unchanged, however, with its round towers and the pump building, once used to water the extensive grounds. The decorative fountains beneath the palace and at the top of the inner arcades have vanished. This notable site is the property of the Municipality of Vienna and restoration work on the palace and the gardens is now underway.

Kaiser-Ebersdorf was mentioned at the beginning of the 12th century as a manorial seat. It passed to Maximilian I by exchange in 1499 and he had it converted into a hunting lodge. Once situated on the heath, the clustered village is still quite separate from the palace complex, of which the church is a part. Due to its isolated position, the place has changed little since the late 19th century. The scene is characterized by village houses, some of them dating back to the baroque and Biedermeier eras. The estate house in the Sellingergasse is remarkable with its arcaded upper storey and the wide sweep of its portal, crowned with figures. The former imperial palace acquired its present appearance when it was rebuilt by Ludovico Burnacini after its destruction in 1683. First mentioned in 1310, the Parish Church has frequently been rebuilt. Behind the church is the Thürnlhof, a lodge said to have served Napoleon as quarters in 1809.

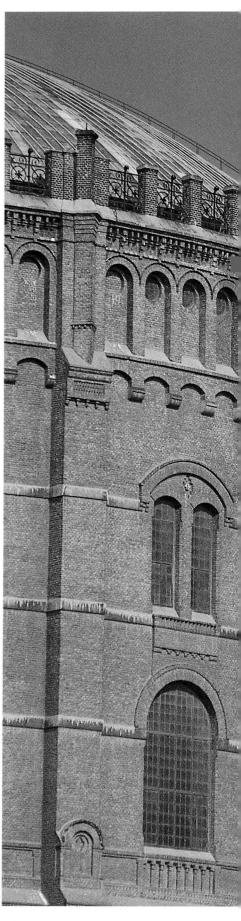

a) Facade of a house on the
"labourers' cottage site",
built in 1896 near the
Anker bread factory in the
Absberggasse
b, c) Industrial area,
Erdberger Mais, with four
gasometers

Neugebäude, outer garden
wall with tower

BETWEEN
THE GÜRTEL
AND THE
VIENNA WOODS

Later called suburbs, the villages outside the ramparts long retained their individuality. The great distance from the city centre and the geographical location impeded amalgamation. Improved traffic conditions in the 19th century meant that these delightfully situated areas became popular summer resorts. The explosive growth in population in the second half of the century made it necessary to enlarge the city again in 1892, only a few decades after the suburbs were first incorporated in the municipality. The ramparts were flattened out, enabling the narrow road that followed the fortification line to be widened, the spacious Gürtelstrasse thus resulting. At the turn of the century other major traffic links were developed — the suburban line from Penzing to Heiligenstadt, crossing the new districts, and the Stadtbahn from Hütteldorf to Heiligenstadt through the Wiental and across the Gürtel and the Danube Canal. Otto Wagner was responsible for the artistic arrangement of these metropolitan railway lines. The underground railway network constituted a further decisive improvement in public transport.

Unlike the suburbs, their old centres swallowed up by the city, the outlying districts have retained their individual character. Large areas of open land in the Vienna Woods and the Viennese basin were also incorporated in the municipality, the city thus acquiring a unique recreation area.

Meidling, the 12th district, extends down the foothills of the Wienerberg, descending south-west between the river Wien and the Liesingbachtal; it comprises the once independent areas of Obermeidling and Untermeidling, Gaudenzdorf and Wilhelmsdorf, as well as Hetzendorf and Altmannsdorf on the northern slopes of the Liesingtal. Meidling itself was mentioned in 1140 as "Murlingen". In the late 18th century Obermeidling developed in the vicinity of the Imperial Palace of

Schönbrunn. It became independent in 1806. Gaudenzdorf, an artisans' settlement, and Wilhelmsdorf, a brickmaking estate, originated in 1819 and 1834 on land belonging to Klosterneuburg Abbey; the names are reminders of Gaudenz Dunkler and Wilhelm Sedlacek, the abbey priors in those years. Of the older boroughs only Altmannsdorf and Hetzendorf have partially retained their rural character. Today, the district is typified by the many council flats and estates built between the Wars and after. The houses at Eichenstrasse 5 to 23 were put up by the Southern Railway Company in 1870 to plans by Wilhelm Flattich. Brick buildings, intended for labourers, their facades are bereft of any articulation, apart from simple cornices. The first council house to be financed from income tax money was the Fuchsenfeldhof (1921/22), planned by Heinrich Schmid and Hermann Aichinger. The buildings are kept relatively close together, only the central section being more spacious. By comparison, the Reismannhof — designed three years later by the same architects — seems a "more modern" solution. The ground-plan is more dispersed, revealing a tendency to monumentalize. The entrance to the Längenfeldgasse is flanked by towerlike, heightened sections which are arranged in arches and loggias at street level.

The first mention of Hetzendorf goes back to 1140, the village probably developing as a row of dwellings; the line of houses in the north must have been added in the late Middle Ages. Between 1456 and 1744 the manor came under the Teutonic Order. In 1694 Franz Sigmund Count of Thun had a hunting lodge built to the east of the village on the site of an estate house; it was extended in 1712 according to plans by Johann Lukas von Hildebrandt. In 1742 the lodge passed to Empress Maria Theresia who commissioned Nikolaus Pacassi to undertake lavish enlargement work. It was then that the avenue connecting it

with Schönbrunn Palace was laid out. Numerous villas were built in the vicinity of the imperial palace. Otherwise, the Hetzendorfer Strasse is characterized by urbanized buildings and late 19th century suburban terraced houses. At the intersection of the Schönbrunner Allee stands the Gallhof, a mansion that was last rebuilt in 1871. Opposite this is the Biedermeier villa in which Hugo Wolf spent the summer of 1876.

First mentioned in 1314, Altmannsdorf developed into a typical triangular village around a green, a form of settlement indicating 11th century origins. The centre is situated away from the Breitenfurter Strasse and thus retained its original essence. The Biedermeier Church of St. Oswald, the focus of the tree-lined Khleslplatz, was built in 1838 on the site of an old chapel and is surrounded by urbanized houses. Sometimes called "Schloss Altmannsdorf", the old estate building belonging to the Augustinian friars is particularly notable. Some of the houses are decorated with sculptures. In front of the church is an oversized statue of St. Augustine and in a niche next to no. 11 is a statue of Johann Nepomuk. With most of its ancient buildings still preserving their original appearance, with its statues and its old trees, the Khleslplatz is one of the most charming village ensembles on the southern periphery of Vienna.

Hietzing, the 13th district, covers an area on the right bank of the Wien in the foothills of the Vienna Woods. The present district boundaries encompass Hacking, Hietzing, Lainz, Speising, Ober and Unter St. Veit and parts of Mauer. The imperial summer residence at Schönbrunn exerted much influence on the development of this area. The palace was erected on the site of a mill belonging to Klosterneuburg Abbey; in 1550 it was converted into a modest mansion and in 1569 it was acquired by Emperor Maximilian II who consequently had it made into a fine hunting lodge.

After its destruction in 1683, the year of the Turkish siege, Johann Bernhard Fischer von Erlach designed the famous imperial summer residence. It was completed in Maria Theresia's reign after several alterations to the plans. The last major conversion was undertaken by Johann Aman between 1816 and 1819. Built around a large, almost square, courtyard, this is one of Austrian baroque's most outstanding achievements. The magnificent grounds were designed by Jean Trehet, the French landscape gardener, in 1705 and were extended by Ferdinand von Hohenberg and Adrian van Steckhoven. Jean Nicolas Jadot de Ville-Issey created the menagerie with the enclosures in a circular arrangement and with the central pavilion. The culmination is the Gloriette, its early classicist, arcaded architecture resembling a stage set. It was completed to Ferdinand von Hohenberg's design in 1775. Other charming focal points are provided by the fountains, the obelisk grotto and the Roman ruins. A natural and an artistic monument, Schönbrunn Palace and the grounds are a historical site of the first order.

First mentioned in 1170, the ownership of Hietzing passed from the Teutonic Order to Klosterneuburg Abbey in exchange for other property. From 1529 onwards pilgrims were attracted to the miraculous image in the Church of the Birth of the Virgin Mary in Hietzing. The construction of the Imperial Summer Residence of Schönbrunn brought tremendous impetus to the area; consequently it became a popular summer resort and a favourite residential district for the rich. Very near to the Palace is the old village centre with the Parish Church and the clustered village along the Altgasse of today; it also encompasses the beginning of the Hietzinger Hauptstrasse. Here, isolated examples of urbanized rural architecture can still be found alongside buildings dating back to the era of Joseph II and Biedermeier country houses. The

quarter between Maxingstrasse, Gloriettegasse and Lainzer Strasse, to the south of the old centre, was developed and built up at the beginning of the 19th century. Numerous Biedermeier houses still survive here, most of them two-storeyed and with a balcony over the porch. In the lower, eastern section of the Maxingstrasse is a row of plain 19th century houses, probably built for artisans and court servants; imposing Biedermeier and late 19th century buildings line the upper section of this street. In the Trauttmannsdorfgasse Biedermeier villas alternate with town houses dating back to the turn of the century, the composition of the acacia-adorned Wattmanngasse is similar. The high Biedermeier building complex in the Gloriettegasse is supplemented by two significant early 20th century buildings — the Villa Schopp by Friedrich Ohmann and Josef Hackhofer and the Haus Primavesi, one of Josef Hoffmann's main works.

The Old People's Home of the Municipality of Vienna at Lainz was built between 1902 and 1904 according to plans by Rudolf Helmreich and Johann Scheiringer. Relieved by plastered sections, the brick pavilions stand on four terraces. Steps lead up to the main group in the centre, its focal point the twin-spired church. This is impressively linked to the administrative blocks by means of single-storey arcades. Planned by Scheiringer and built between 1908 and 1913, the neighbouring hospital is more compact, four elongated wings of different design enclosing a courtyard with a fountain in the centre. The eye is caught by the little tower of the chapel in the west wing, which forms the rear elevation of the courtyard. The Hermeswiese council estate was built in 1923/24 according to plans by Karl Ehn. Crowned by a little clock tower, the entrance in the Hochmaisgasse gives access to the Lynkeusgasse which is lined by loose groups of houses, the brick doorway surrounds their sole ornamentation. The high

hipped roofs — they are sometimes gabled — with their flat tiles feature small dormer windows. The estate is situated on the main approach to Lainz Zoological Gardens, which extend well into the Vienna Woods. It was in this beautiful park that Carl Hasenauer built the Hermesvilla for Empress Elizabeth. Near the Zoo, between Veitingergasse and Jagdschlossgasse, a model estate of small single family houses was put up for the Viennese *Werkbund* Exhibition of 1932 as an example of modern architecture. The initiator was Josef Frank, the architect, who proposed the names of 33 other architects of note; they included Jacques Groag, Josef Hoffmann, Clemens Holzmeister, Ernst Lichtblau, Adolf Loos, Oskar Strnad, Hugo Häring (Germany), Richard J. Neutra (United States of America), Gerrit Rietveld (Holland) and André Lurçat (France). Each was invited to realize his own concept within certain guide-lines, simplicity and economy being the order of the day. Despite the limitations imposed by the concept as a whole, the seventy houses reveal the personal style of their creators. The site planning is also of interest, being inspired by the English garden cities of that time and catering to new social trends. Most of the buildings are still preserved more or less in their original state.

Ober St. Veit developed from a church hamlet, first mentioned in 1195 between Firmiangasse and Glasauergasse. In 1365 Duke Rudolf IV ceded the manor house to the cathedral authority of All Saints at St. Stephen's. As from 1480 the entire manor was the property of the bishopric. In 1742 Bishop Kollonitz had the old manor house converted into a summer residence. The rustic character of the old lanes has been preserved, the wine-growers' houses later being made into dairy farms. The entire scene and the surroundings are dominated by the church in its elevated position and by the archbishop's residence.

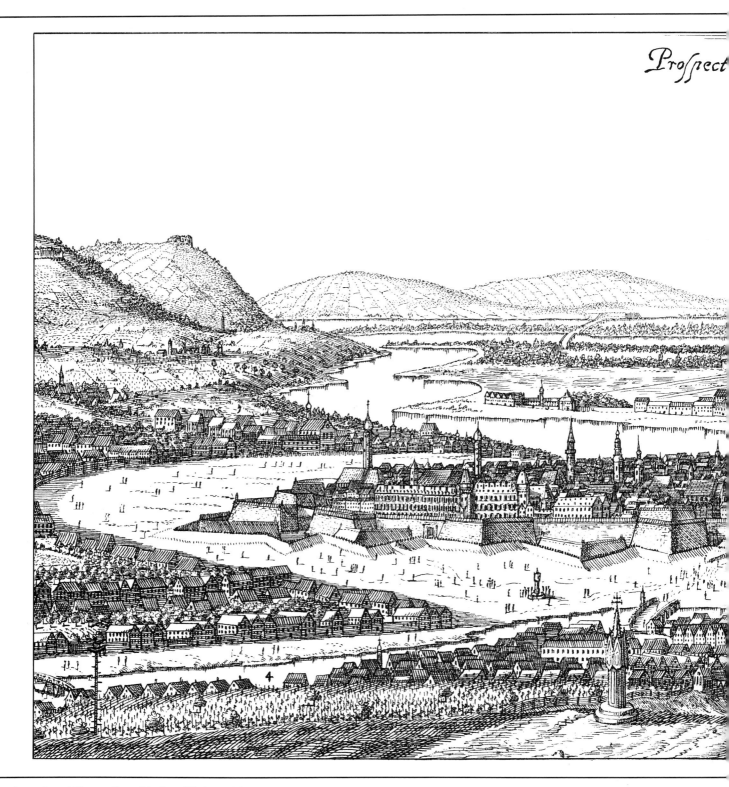

Southern view of Vienna, Georg Matthäus Vischer, 1672

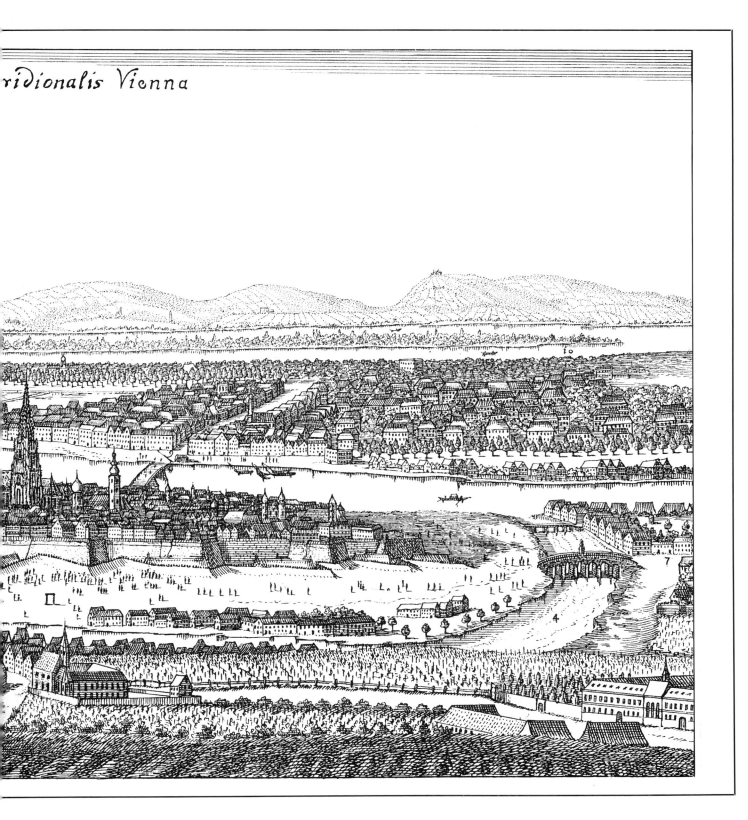

ridionalis Vienna

In 1938 that part of the 13th district north of the river Wien (with the old hamlets of Baumgarten, Breitensee, Hütteldorf and Penzing) was merged with Hadersdorf-Weidlingau — this including the ornate baroque Parish Church of Mariabrunn and the Augustine monastery — to form **Penzing,** the 14th district. This extends from the wooded heights of the Vienna Woods to the Schmelzterrasse. All the various phases of urbanization can be observed here, untouched woodland and loosely built-up garden estates alternating with industrial areas and densely built housing estates, in particular nearer to the city alongside the railway line. Mentioned in 1120, Penzing probably developed in the 9th century on the ancient Roman road that crossed the river at a ford here. The oldest settlement presumably consisted of a row of houses between Diesterweggasse and Einwanggasse. In the 18th century Penzing became a popular summer resort and it was then that the first silk factories became established here. In Biedermeier days a quiet, middle class residential area developed, the Penzinger Strasse being an example of this. Old rustic buildings brush shoulder here with baroque, classicist and Biedermeier summer houses belonging to the aristocracy and the bourgeoisie and with numerous late 19th century apartment blocks with elaborately articulated facades. The winding course of the road and the irregular houses of different periods give a delightfully picturesque effect. An estate for artisans employed at Schönbrunn was situated on the left of the Einwanggasse, which leads to the Parish Church of St. James. Today, this road is dominated by elegant art nouveau facades. In the square in front of the church a remnant of the old cemetery can be seen — a late Gothic lantern-post with a relief design depicting the Crucifixion. The Hadikgasse did not develop until the second half of the 19th century, the top section featuring harmonious

groups of villas with front gardens. The mansion at no. 72, with its striking tower, served as Richard Wagner's residence in 1863/64. Hütteldorf was mentioned in 1156/71 as "Utendorf". In 1356 Wernhard Schenk, the ducal forester, established the parish. The mediaeval settlement soon developed into a modest village along a single street. Rebuilt after its destruction in the Turkish siege of 1683, it became a popular summer resort in the early 19th century and an urban residential district as from the turn of the century. Biedermeier country houses and villas are to be found here alongside the scant remains of the village settlement and late 19th century apartment blocks, among them the late baroque Miller-Aichholz mansion with outbuildings and extensive grounds, the Windischgrätz villa at no. 452 and the former summer house of the hospitallers at no. 466.

The Trinity Column by the new Parish Church (1881/82) was moved from the centre of the road to the wall a few years ago. In the Hüttelbergstrasse, in a wooded property at the foot of the Hüttelberg, are two adjacent villas (nos. 26 and 28) built by Otto Wagner for his own use. Now the property of Ernst Fuchs, the graphic artist and painter, the older building dates back to 1886 and features Renaissance forms with an open, pillared portico and pergolas. The other house was built in 1913, a cubic building of reinforced concrete with an overhanging cornice and mosaics by Kolo Moser.

The Steinhof Psychiatric Hospital was built between 1950 and 1907 on the slopes of the Gallitzinberg. Comprised of 34 pavilions, the site was planned by Franz Berger and Carlo von Boog, the church (1913) being by Otto Wagner. From the Flötzersteig a wide approach road leads up to the main axis of the asylum. Originally the female patients were housed to the left and the men on the right, the buildings being surrounded by green

expanses and having access via a system of winding paths. Vienna's most outstanding sacred building in the art noveau style, Otto Wagner's Church of St. Leopold forms an imposing conclusion. Originally designed for wealthy patients, the group of asylum buildings in the west acquired a separate function in 1923 when the Baumgartner Höhe Sanatorium was installed there.

Documents of 1195 mention Breitensee, its name derived from the pond of the village centre which disappeared in the last century. The oval shaped village grew up along an old route connecting Ottakring and Penzing, the Kendlerstrasse of today. Until the 19th century vineyards were a part of the scene here. Brickworks took their place and Breitensee became a workmen's suburb. The new buildings are spaciously planned; the old village green became a suburban square in the style of the turn of the century, some remnants of the original village buildings surviving. The neo-Gothic Parish Church of St. Laurence to the east of the old green was built according to plans by Ludwig Zatzka. The buildings in the church square are late 19th century apartment blocks.

Rudolfsheim-Fünfhaus, the 15th district, extends from the Schmelz to the river Wien. The older villages declined during the wars with the Hungarians and the Turks at the beginning of the modern era and settlement did not recommence until after the second Turkish siege. Founded at that time, the artisans's and tradesmen's settlements of Reindorf and Rustendorf were merged with Braunhirschengrund in 1863 to form the suburb of Rudolfsheim. Formed in 1938 by amalgamating the 14th and 15th district, the 15th district of today comprises the old suburban communes of Sechshaus, Rudolfsheim and Fünfhaus. In the late 19th century the southern half of the district — it is divided by the western railway line — was inhabited mainly by weavers and many textile firms can still be found in the area today; industrialization led to the establishment of large workmen's estates. A typical example of a simple sacred building in the era of Joseph II, Reindorf Parish Church of the Holy Trinity was erected in 1786. Fünfhauser Parish Church was built in 1867/69 according to plans by Friedrich Schmidt; an imposing neo-Gothic domed building, it still dominates the Mariahilfer Gürtel, where it is visible from afar. The north-east section of the district was not built up until the turn of the century. A huge parade ground extended this far and building was prohibited until 1894. A cemetery took up part of the terrain; laid out during Joseph II's reign, it was the burial site of those killed in the March revolution of 1848. The cemetery was closed in 1908, a park taking its place. An ambitious venture in urban planning, the "Nibelungen" quarter between Gablenzgasse, Vogelweidplatz and Hütteldorfer Strasse was built up in 1910, its apartment houses featuring art nouveau facade decorations. In the eastern section of the Kriemhildplatz is Clemens Holzmeister's Church of Christ the King (1933) with its rectory centre built around an inner courtyard. The buildings in the Hütteldorfer Strasse and Wurzbachgasse mostly date back to the period between the Wars; the massive complex of the second Trade School of Further Education is a representative example of the monumental style of public buildings during the Twenties. Leopold Bauer's Vogelweidhof was built in 1926 and is remarkable on account of its arcades with their fresco ornamentation by Rudolf Jettmayr and Franz Wacik. The Stadthalle opposite was built between 1953 and 1958 according to Roland Rainer's design.

Ottakring, the 16th district, is situated on the upper course of the Ottakringerbach and comprises Ottakring and Neulerchenfeld, a workmen's estate that developed in around 1700 and that was separated from the Lerchenfeld area when the fortification line was erected. During the period of industrialization in the late 19th century extensive estates developed, the appearance of the uniform blocks of flats being enlivened by wide roads, some of them laid out as avenues. Thanks to its situation on the slopes of the Vienna Woods, the area has become a coveted residential district in recent years.

The oldest settlement centre around Alt-St.-Lambert in the area of the Gallitzinstrasse — Johann Staud-Gasse was destroyed in 1683. The later settlement can still be recognized in the top section of the Ottakringer Strasse, but otherwise the old wine-growing village has completely disappeared, apart from a few scanty remains of buildings. In 1884 Moriz v. Kuffner, the industrialist, had an observatory constructed here. In 1905 a palace was built on the nearby Gallizinberg or Wilhelminenberg for Archduke Leopold Salvator, it was later converted into a children's home and then into a hotel. The old Parish Church in Ottakring was replaced in 1910 by Rudolf Wiskoczil's new building. Work on the extensive Sandleiten apartment block started in 1924, various architects being involved in the planning. The aim was a picturesque arrangement in the style of Camillo Sitte. The various wings are loosely arranged around irregular courtyards and squares and differ from one another in their facades. On the other side of the Rosenackerstrasse a separate group of smaller premises were built with delightfully ornamented plaster surfaces. The Church of St. Joseph was built in 1935/36 according to plans by Josef Vytiska. A truly modern touch came to the Herbststrasse in 1911 with Schmelz Parish Church, a reinforced concrete building, devoid of any spire. It was designed by Josef Plecnik.

Hernals, the 17th district, corresponds geographically to the upper catchment area of the Alserbach. Arched over, this flows beneath the Alszeile, Hernalser Hauptstrasse and Jörgerstrasse and comprises the old villages of Hernals, Dornbach and Neuwaldegg. The fields here were densely built up with apartment blocks in the late 19th century, but some of the adjacent vineyards still remain. Along the periphery, rows of villas stretch as far as the edge of the Vienna Woods.

The village on the banks of the Alsbach was first mentioned in 1302 as "Herrenals", whilst the area by the lower course of the stream was called Siechenals. In 1587 — at that time the district was the centre of Viennese Protestantism — Hernals passed to the Jörger dynasty. After they were outlawed in 1620, the manor passed to the cathedral chapter of Vienna as an imperial fief. In the course of the Counter-Reformation a "Holy Grave" was erected next to the old Parish Church of St. Bartholomew and as from 1639 it was the destination of a pilgrimage procession from St. Stephen's. One of the stages of the Cross has been preserved at the corner of the Alserstrasse and the Schlösselgasse, it depicts Christ before Annas, the high priest. In 1709 a Calvary hill and a church were built in Hernals and looked after by the Pauline Order. Once the site of the Jörger castle, St. Bartholomäusplatz is dominated by the Calvary Church; this was renovated in 1894.

Dating back to the 12th century, Dornbach was for many years the property of the Benedictine Abbey of St. Peter in Salzburg, which still takes care of the parish today. Viticulture flourished here in every era. In the 19th century the place became a popular summer resort. Its centre followed the same course as the Alsbach, although this has since been regulated and now flows under the Alszeile. Little remains of the original village buildings; late 19th century suburban terraced houses and villas predominate, some of them with front gardens. The site of the Parish Church, the rectory and former farm buildings belonging to St. Peter's Abbey, Rupertusplatz is situated away from the traffic and provides a pleasantly rural touch. A hamlet called Ober-Dornbach once belonged to Dornbach. Neuwaldegg palace, now a Catholic education centre, was built by Johann Bernhard Fischer von Erlach between 1692 and 1697 for Count Theodor Strattmann. In 1765 Field Marshal Moritz Count Lacy acquired the property and had a landscape garden laid out here, the first "English" park in Austria. Neuwaldegg, a settlement in a clearing, only numbered ten houses in 1760, but the public Lacy gardens brought tremendous impetus. A very few villas in the Neuwaldegger Strasse provide a continuing reminder of the early days. In 1908 the early 18th century Chapel of St. Anne was moved to its present site for traffic considerations.

Above Dornbach, the Heuberg estate was the work of Adolf Loos who was intensively involved with area planning after the First World War, holding the post of chief architect to the estate office of the Municipality of Vienna from 1920 to 1922. Loos himself designed one row of houses here, but his ideas were not fully realized in the other houses. The construction of the buildings is based mainly on his patented idea of the "house with one wall": wooden front and back walls are inserted between side walls arranged in a row. Intended for those returning from the War and for invalids, the estate consists of two-storeyed terrace houses with flat roofs. The watershed of a stream, the Währinger Bach, also determined the development of **Währing,** the 18th district, which comprises Währing, Weinhaus, Gersthof and Pötzleinsdorf. Hardly touched by 19th century industrialization, the district is a residential area, densely built up as far as the suburban railway line, whilst the sections on the periphery are

interspersed with large green areas. First mentioned in 1170, Währing at that time belonged to the Salzburg Benedictine Abbey of Michelbeuern. Even in the late Middle Ages the double row of houses extended along the bank of the Währinger Bach to the Aumannplatz of today. The elongated village was destroyed during the Hungarian invasion under Matthias Corvinus, who set up one of his three camps here in 1485. The place was divided when the fortification line was erected. The area within the wall was later incorporated in the 9th district. In the late 19th century the suburb became a residential area, the old houses disappeared, the layout of the village was altered, the fields divided into plots and access provided by a road network. The old centre can still be recognized in the course of the Währinger Strasse and Gentzgasse. One of the last relics of the rural past is the former Währing Cemetery with its Empire style portal; now a park, it contains the graves of Beethoven and Schubert. The cottage house in the area Haitzingergasse—Anton Frank-Gasse—Weimarerstrasse—Cottagegasse date back to the first phase of building here. Small villas with several storeys, loosely dispersed in the English manner, they were inspired by Heinrich Ferstel and built by the Wiener Cottage Verein, a society founded in 1872. Intended for the less affluent, the earliest of these cottage houses were modest in design. To the west of the cottage estate are large parks: the Sternwartepark is named after the observatory designed by Ferdinand Fellner and Hermann Helmer and erected here in 1874/78; the Türkenschanzpark was opened in 1888. Opposite this stands the University of Agriculture which was built in 1896 and enlarged on several occasions.

The village of Gersthof probably developed around a sizeable farm estate mentioned in the late 15th century. As from 1444 the Gerstlerhof belonged to the Dorotheerkloster, a

convent, and it passed to Klosterneuburg Abbey in 1782. The private Chapel of St. John of Nepomuk became the Parish Church in 1784. Today, the rural part of the Gersthofer Strasse is only discernible in the area of the little church, in the vicinity of which are the former benefice house at no. 129, several urbanized farmsteads and the baroque hunting lodge at no. 143. The area to the south of the old centre acquired its road network at the end of the 19th century. The Provincial Central Children's Home (now the Semmelweis Clinic) was built in the grounds of the former Gersthof manor house between 1908 and 1910.

Pötzleinsdorf village developed along a road and was first mentioned in 1112. From 1455 to 1571 the manor was owned by the Dorotheerkloster and it later became the property of the Himmelpfortkloster. In 1797 Johann Heinrich Geymüller purchased the property and had it converted into a representational mansion. The adjacent area on the north-east slope of the Schafberg was laid out as a large landscape garden to Rosenthal's design; the evenue leading from Gersthof to the entrance to the mansion also dates back to that period. The wine-growing village was almost completely destroyed by fire in 1750. Like many other suburbs on the edge of the Vienna Woods, Pötzleinsdorf became a popular summer resort in the 19th century. The original wine growers' houses at street level on the south side of Pötzleinsdorfer Strasse are still mainly intact, summer houses were built on the north side in the 19th century. These houses and the front gardens are set above street level, only being accessible via steep steps. High garden walls are a feature of this street and of the Khevenhüllerstrasse with its 18th and 19th century country houses. The baroque Parish Church of St. Giles commands the crossroads, an old avenue of chestnut-trees leading up to it; opposite this is the Geymüllerschlösschen, a country house dating back to the Empire period and remarkable on account of its neo-Gothic and Egyptian-like decorations.

Döbling, the 19th district with its particularly delightful scenery, extends as far as the ridge of the Vienna Woods as they fall away steeply to the Danube. The old villages all developed in the valleys of four streams. The entire area was once dominated by the castle (1280) on the Leopoldsberg — or Kahlenberg, as it was then called — and the last remains of this are situated next to the Church of St. Leopold. The major road today is the Heiligenstädter Strasse which leads north along the Danube, forming the boundary between the industrial quarter on the bank of the Danube Canal and the residential areas which are still characterized by the centres of the old wine-growing villages. The villages scattered along the periphery extend as far as the vineyards on the edge of the Vienna Woods.

Mentioned as ''Topilicha'' in 1115, the settlement on the old arterial road on the south bank of the Danube is divided into Ober and Unter Döbling by Krottenbach stream. From the 12th to the 14th century the village belonged to the lords of Döbling and then it passed to the convent of Dominican nuns in Tulln, remaining in their possession for four centuries. The original settlement forms have more or less entirely disappeared. As from the late 18th century several aristocratic country seats were built in the old wine-growing village, Field Marshal Daun's mansion at Hofzeile 20 being one example. Subsequently a rural village community developed, later becoming a grand urban residential area. Döbling Parish Church was completed in its present form in 1829; a delightful group of two-storey Biedermeier country houses in the Billrothstrasse also dates back to that period. In the Döblinger Hauptstrasse — this follows the route of the Roman *limes* — are the remains

of the Casino Zögernitz (1837) and several neighbouring country houses, as well as the former St. John of Nepomuk Chapel on the corner of the Hofzeile. The Villa Wertheimstein is set in large grounds and was built by Ludwig Pichl in 1836 for Rudolf von Arthaber. In 1867 it passed to the Wertheimstein family whose salon was a meeting-point for scholars and artists of note.

The settlement of Neustift am Walde on the northern bank of Krottenbach stream was first mentioned in 1330. In 1413 the manor was acquired by Andreas Plank, chancellor to Duke Albrecht V and parish priest at Gars; it was conveyed to the Dorotheerkloster in Vienna as a prebend. In 1749 the wine-growing village still only numbered 23 houses. In the late 19th century small terraced houses and villas were added, but most of the rural buildings and gabled wine-growers' houses have been preserved in the northern row. On the slope, in the corner between Rathstrasse and the steep road up to Pötzleinsdorf is the little village church of St. Rochus, dating back to 1851 in its present form.

The little wine-growing village of Salmannsdorf was first mentioned in 1279. Situated on a mountain slope at an altitude of 300 metres, the manor was for many years the property of Klosterneuburg Abbey. A popular summer resort in the 19th century, this is a select residential area where wine-growing still plays a part. Village buildings can still be found in the tree-lined Dreimarktsteingasse, together with low terraced houses built in the late 19th century. From 1829 to 1836 the Strauss family spent the summer months in house no. 13. Next to no. 12, probably the oldest building in Salmannsdorf, is a little 18th century chapel.

The elongated village of Sievering was first mentioned in 1114. Twenty years later it passed to Klosterneuburg Abbey, a gift by the ruler. After several changes in ownership the place

was divided in 1634, Ober-Sievering being acquired by the Camaldulites and Unter-Sievering by Gaming Charterhouse. The church hamlets around St. Severin and a clustered village at the fork of Sieveringer Strasse and Agnesgasse were probably the oldest centres of settlement. Most of the buildings in the lower section of the district — country houses, villas, isolated apartment houses and new houses — date back to the mid-19th century. The general scene is particularly pleasing with the many old trees. The upper part is extensively untouched and has retained its village character. Here, on both sides of the narrowing Sieveringer Strasse and in the lower section of the Agnesgasse is a compact group of winegrowers' houses, some of them with gabled street fronts. One of the oldest is the house at Agnesgasse 1, once a farm building belonging to the Camaldulites. In Unter-Sievering there are still remains of the original rural buildings, but 19th century houses predominate.

The Kaasgraben colony of villas was built for artists and their families between 1912 and 1914 on the initiative of Yella Hertzka, a champion of women's rights. Planned by Josef Hoffmann, the two-storey buildings loosely grouped around a green are characterized by a simplicity of style. The whole effect is determined by the large windows with small divisions, wide defined cornices and high roofs. First mentioned in 1114, Grinzing, the village on the Nesselbach, was described as a flourishing settlement in the Klosterneuburg Abbey records in the 12th century. In the Middle Ages various bishoprics and abbeys owned property here. The fortified Trummelhof — it still exists today — was endowed on Seyfried Reichold of Grinzing in the 14th century. Another old estate is the Pöltingerhof. As from the 18th century the place developed into a popular excursion site. Today, Grinzing and its many ''Heurigen'' taverns are a particular tourist attraction; it is also an exclusive residential area. The centre of the old village has in essence been preserved and consists of wine-growers' houses of different eras, surrounded by 19th and 20th century houses and villas. With its baroque onion dome, the late Gothic church provides a special touch, so does the green with its little chapel.

The Karl Marx Hof in the Heiligenstädter Strasse was built between 1927 and 1930 according to plans by Karl Ehn, Otto Wagner's pupil. The elongated estate comprises 1,325 flats and is regarded as a model of communal housing between the Wars. Monotony was intentionally avoided here by the use of different colours and arrangements. Forming the conclusion of a wide, park-like forecourt, the imposing central section is plastically arranged with massive arches and rhythmic projections, an "expressive" monumental effect being the aim.

Heiligenstadt was first mentioned in 1120/25 as *apud Sanctum Michaelem* and, later, *apud Sanctum Locum*. Restored between 1894 and 1898, the Parish Church of St. Michael stands at the point where the old Roman *limes* crossed Nestelbach stream. The name of the place is said to derive from St. Severin who worked in the area, preaching to heathens, and who is said to be buried here. Branching off eastwards from the *limes*, the Probusgasse leads to the Romanesque Church of St. James in the Pfarrplatz. The place started to flourish in the late 18th century, the mineral spring discovered in 1781 becoming a special attraction. Among the numerous summer visitors were Beethoven, Grillparzer, Schubert and Schwind. After the spring dried up, the grounds of the bathing house were acquired by the Municipality and converted into public gardens. Here, too, the buildings date back to the 18th and 19th century. Uniform groups of old wine growers' houses can still be found in Probusgasse, Eroicagasse and

Armbrustergasse. The old church forms a picturesque group with the baroque rectory and rural buildings. Here and in the Probusgasse there are sites commemorating Beethoven. Nussdorf was first mentioned in 1114 and probably grew up from several little settlements on the *limes*. Wine-growing also provided the foundation of Nussdorf's affluence, 15 such estates once existing here. The ratchet railway up to the Kahlenberg was a particular attraction in the 19th century. The old buildings — mostly urbanized wine-growers' homes — have been extensively preserved and the Kahlenberger Strasse is a well kept example of a wine growing settlement in the west of Vienna. One and two-storey gabled houses, many of them dating back to the 16th and 17th century, predominate in the northern row. In the summer of 1824 Beethoven lived at no. 26, a house with an ornate rococo arrangement. In the Hackhofergasse manorial buildings prevail, examples being the massive complex of the former Altenburg mansion of the Zwettlerhof with its splendid baroque facade. Of particular note is the Schikaneder mansion with its large terrace garden, Franz Lehár's home from 1932 to 1944. The Greinergasse leads from the Nussdorfer Platz to the Hackhofergasse and southwards in a curve. The row of houses on each side of the simple church form a charmingly rural group.

Nussdorf weir and the administrative building on the Brigittenauer Spitz were built between 1894 and 1898 according to plans by Otto Wagner. With its monumental lion pylons, the lock forms a representational gateway to the city.

Kahlenbergdorf dates back to a foundation during the Babenberger era. A Chapel of St. George existed here until the 13th century and was mentioned as early as 1168. Kahlenbergdorf was fortified in the later Middle Ages, being called an *oppidum* in 1487. As from the 15th century the

wine-growing village was also an important stage for the salt trade on the Danube. The Parish Church of St. George — in its present form it goes back to the 17th century — dominates the village with its imposing 17th and 18th century wine-growers' homes, some of them older still in essence. This ancient place with its narrow, winding streets is particularly charming on account of its position between the Danube and the gentle vine-covered slopes. The Leopoldsberg and the Kahlenberg can be reached from here. A Camaldulite hermitage was founded on this spur of the Vienna Woods in 1628 by Emperor Ferdinand II and several small houses and the church still provide a reminder of the original monastery.

Liesing, the 23rd district, has belonged to Vienna since 1938, the present boundary dating back to a regulation of 1946 which was enforced in 1954. The district extends from the Vienna Woods on both sides of the Liesingbach to the Viennese basin and it comprises the once independent villages of Atzgersdorf, Erlaa, Inzersdorf, Kalksburg, Liesing (created a town in 1903), Mauer, Rodaun and Siebenhirten. Most of these villages developed along old routes, like the Liesinger Weg that ran from Mariahilf via the Meidlinger Sattel and Liesing to Perchtoldsdorf and the road from Hietzing to Lainz and Perchtoldsdorf. Spread between the old village is an industrial area which is intersected by the road and the railway and interspersed with residential districts and agricultural land.

Mauer lies on the old road from the Wiental across the Lainzer Sattel, the name perhaps being derived from the remains of a Roman wall. At the intersection of Lange Gasse and Kaserngasse a fortress once protected the road and the ruler's hunting ground from attack. In the Biedermeier period Mauer was an elegant summer resort and further impetus came in 1883 with the opening of the steam tramway from Hietzing to Perchtoldsdorf. Once of importance, wine-growing declined and finally ceased due to building development and the village lost its rural character. Next to Clemens Holzmeister's Parish Church — built in 1935/37, this incorporated an old chapel — in the northern row of the Endresstrasse is an early classicist mansion with an estate building. Towering up on the knoll of St. Georgenberg and visible from afar, stands the concrete Church of the Trinity, built between 1974 and 1976 to a design by Fritz Wotruba, the sculptor.

Rodaun was first mentioned in 1170 and grew up as a hamlet at the foot of the mediaeval fortress on a slope in the Liesingtal. An early wine-growing centre and a popular summer resort in the Biedermeier period, the clustered village now consists mainly of 19th century country houses and urbanized farmsteads. Several old buildings remain in the Ketzergasse: an old inn (no. 465), the doorway keystone bearing the date 1577, and a baroque mansion built in 1724 for Prince Trautson and later acquired by Empress Maria Theresia for Countess Fuchs, her governess. Hugo von Hofmannsthal lived here from 1901 until his death in 1929. Visible from afar, the baroque church dominates the scene from its commanding position on the wooded mountain ridge. The approach is flanked by oversized figures of saints. In a tree-filled park at the end of the Willergasse stands the old castle, now a convent school, with a mediaeval circular tower and a Renaissance doorway, the magnificent classicist facade facing the steep slope.

Kalksburg grew up out of a church hamlet beneath the castle belonging to the Chalsbperger, first mentioned in 1235. In 1609 the village was endowed on the Jesuits and after the order was suppressed it passed to Franz von Mack, the court jeweller. In 1856 the Jesuits again acquired the property from his heirs and they built the existing seminary here. The area is dominated by the neo-classical church, an arcaded passage giving access to the rectory below. Visitors approaching from the east have a charming view through the arch of the church square and its loose group of mainly rural buildings.

First mentioned in 1125, Inzersdorf developed around a green by the Liesingbach. The brick industry in the neighbourhood — quarrying went on here in Roman times — flourished tremendously in the 19th century and this had an adverse effect on the old village buildings. The Hochwassergasse on the bank of the Liesing does, however, still feature some rural buildings. The little baroque manor house (no. 38) dating back to the 18th century provides a gracious focal point, its old garden wall the site of a statue of St. John of Nepomuk. The Parish Church of St. Nicholas (c. 1820), a circular neo-classical building, is also remarkable.

Atzgersdorf was first mentioned in 1120. A plain building dating back to the era of Joseph II in its present form, the Parish Church of St. Catherine was a fortified church and the centre of a parish in around 1300. Many of the surrounding places — including Liesing, Erlaa and Siebenhirten — belonged to this parish. There are but few reminders of the days before these areas were industrialized and urbanized, they include Schloss Liesing, now a nursing home belonging to the Municipality of Vienna, or Schloss Alterlaa, its present appearance dating back to 1770; in the extensive grounds are the remains of an artificial ruin and a small circular temple. Opposite this rococo-like aristocratic residence are three terraced high-rise buildings which were erected in the 1970s, each of them containing over 1,000 flats.

Hernals Village, Merian 1649

Schönbrunn:
a) the newly restored
palm-house
b) Right side portal of
the main entrance
c) Garden front of the
palace

Page 126/127:
a) Gloriette,
b) Naiad Fountain
c) wistaria in flower in
the "Kammergarten"
d) Central pavilion of the
menagerie

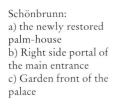

c

d

a) 13, Gloriettegasse 9, villa by Josef Hoffmann
b) 14, Hüttelbergstrasse 26, villa by Otto Wagner
c) 14, Baumgartner Höhe 1, St. Leopold am Steinhof by Otto Wagner, the interior of the asylum church. Altar mosaics by Remigius Geyling, Rudolf Jettmar and Leopold Forstner

b

c

129

Werkbund estate by
Josef Hoffmann and
André Lurçat;
13, Veitingergasse

a

b

c

d

a — d Grinzing

a

a) Window of a house in
Sievering
b) Vineyards in late
autumn; in the
background, the
Kaasgrabenkirche

b

19, Heiligenstädter Strasse,
Karl Marx-Hof

Page 138/139:
On the Kahlenberg

ON THE OTHER BANK OF THE DANUBE

Floridsdorf, the 21st district, is geographically a part of the Marchfeld. It was created in 1904, originally comprising the greater borough of Floridsdorf and the area that is today the 22nd district. Until the course of the Danube was regulated, these places were difficult to reach. Situated on the alluvium of the Danube and constantly endangered, the area was settled in prehistoric days; in the Roman era it lay outside the imperial boundaries, on the other side of the *limes*. In the 9th and 10th centuries it was a part of the kingdom of Great Moravia. Most of the existing settlements date back to 11th and 12th century foundations, but some of the mediaeval places became desolate after flooding and later disappeared. Urban

development commenced at the end of the 18th century, when the prior of Klosterneuburg Abbey made land available here for would-be settlers. The regulation of the Danube determined further development. 475 metres wide and provided with high flood barriers, the inundation area secured the area on the left bank of the Danube. Protection from flooding was recently improved by the excavation of a second river bed as a relief channel. The earlier regulation work provided the population with a swimming paradise and the second created the "Donauinsel", an island between the main course of the river and the "New Danube", another ideal recreation area.

Its geographical position favourable to

factory sites, Floridsdorf soon became an industrial district. The imposing town hall built in 1901 is a reminder of the greater borough of yore. It has served as district headquarters since 1904. At the beginning of this century a group of houses were built in the Prager Strasse for the Mautner-Markhof family who owned breweries here. Neo-baroque in style, they enliven the local scene with their areas of green. The Anton Schlinger Hof site was built by the council in 1925/26 to plans by Hans Glaser and Karl Scheffel. The monumental main facade which encompasses Floridsdorf market is accentuated by the "gate tower" above the main entrance and enlivened by lunettes in relief and by oriels. The Karl Seitz Hof was built

View of Vienna from the Bisamberg, Friedrich Loos 1845

The Danube water meadows seen from Nussdorf, Viennese painter, late 18th century

for the council between 1926 and 1933 by Hubert Gassner, a pupil of Otto Wagner's. In the west the site forms a wide exedra which culminates in the huge portal. This monumental architecture is continued in the symmetric main axis with its network of large park-like courtyards. The church behind the building was erected in 1964 and features a campanile-like tower in the shape of a tapering pyramid.

Mentioned in 1120/25 as "Ucinse", Jedlesee was first encountered under this name in 1530. Situated on a branch of the Danube by the crossing to Nussdorf, the area was constantly endangered by flooding. Until 1728 the road to Prague also ran this way. Around the old village square with the Parish Church of Maria Loretto (1713) and the manor house (later the rectory) belonging to Klosterneuburg Abbey are the remains of rural and suburban 19th century buildings. Gross Jedlersdorf on the Brünner Strasse was mentioned in 1150 as "Urliugestorf". Essentially, the buildings here date back to the 19th century, the place having been destroyed in the wars with the Turks and the French. Urbanized farmsteads which have retained their village character predominate, between these stand new buildings of one to three storeys. A partially renewed baroque building, the rural Parish Church of St. Karl Borromäus stands in the middle of the main street. Traffic to Brno passed this way until 1728.

Stammersdorf on the slopes of the Bisamberg to the west of the Brünner Strasse was first mentioned in around 1180. Hardly altered, the groups of village buildings consist of farmhouses and late 19th century single storey terraced houses, some of which have retained their historicist facade. On the village green stands a column dedicated to the Virgin Mary and several stone statues of saints. The rectory (1690) in the middle of the village — it features a large baroque doorway — leads to the Church of St. Nicholas, set in a slightly elevated position on the outskirts. Baroquified and enlarged in the 19th century, this was once a fortified church. West of the village, the Hagenbrunner Strasse and Krottenhofgasse feature compact rows of wine cellars and lead to the vineyards on the Bisamberg. Leopoldau, an elongated village on a gravel bed in the Danube, was first mentioned in 1120 as "Alpiltowe". Its present appearance took shape in various stages of development. The old layout still exists, so do some of the old single-storey buildings, their facades renovated at the turn of the century; the small apartment blocks date back to the same period. The baroquified Parish Church and the imposing estate house belonging to Klosterneuburg Abbey (1677) stand in the centre, this has retained its village atmosphere thanks to the trees and the parklike green. To the north of this area is the Grossfeldsiedlung, a high-rise estate built between 1966 and 1973.

Donaustadt, the 22nd district, was formed in 1938, composed of the eastern section of Floridsdorf, together with Aspern, Hirschstetten, Kagran, Stadlau, the Marchfeld communes of Breitenlee, Essling and Süssenbrunn, Kaisermühlen and thirteen Lower Austrian communes. It was given the name Gross-Enzersdorf. The present boundaries were not finally regulated until 1954, when Gross-Enzersdorf and other areas were again detached from the district. Covering an area of 102 sq. km., Donaustadt is the largest district of Vienna and is larger than districts I to XI together. It does, however, contain large expanses of land used for agriculture and market gardening; it was not until recent decades that a huge complex of apartment blocks was built on open land here. The Lobau with its water meadows is one of Vienna's most popular recreation areas.

Süssenbrunn was mentioned in 1200 when it belonged to the Schottenstift. It acquired its name in the 16th century from a landowner called Urban Suess. The "Schloss" built in the 19th century on the site of an ancient fortified farmstead is, in fact, a Biedermeier manor-house belonging to the

Theresian Academy. Breitenlee fell into decay after destruction by the Turks in 1529 and was not re-founded until 1695, when it acquired an orthogonal layout. The single-storey village buildings have all been preserved, even if the facades have frequently been altered. The focal point of the interesting group is the Parish Church of St. Anne (1699) and the imposing manor-house belonging to the Schottenstift, its baroque doorway bearing the date 1698.

Hirschstetten was named as "Hertstetten" in 1240. In 1713 the manor was acquired by Prince Adam Franz Schwarzenberg, who had the mansion there magnificently rebuilt by Anton Martinelli. Latterly owned by the von Pirquet family, it was destroyed in the Second World War, only the chapel and the garden gateway surviving. The older buildings in the village are still intact, but most of the facades have been renewed; at the western exit of the village at no. 74 is a baroque chapel of St. John of Nepomuk with a flourishing gable.

Aspern was mentioned in 1258. Once edged by the Wimpffengasse, Siegesplatz and Gross-Enzersdorfer Strasse, the village green has been built up. The place acquired historic renown with the Battle of Aspern on 21st and 22nd May, 1809, when it was more or less totally destroyed; at the corner of Ehrensteingasse-Wimpffengasse a picturesque rural group surrounds the baroque statue of St. Florian. In front of the Church of St. Martin stands an imposing monument, Anton Fernkorn's lion of Aspern (1858); in the area of the former cemetery is the old Chapel of St. Sebastian, now the site of the "Aspern 1809" Museum. Mentioned in around 1250, Essling probably developed in mediaeval times beside the Eslarn family estate. In the 17th and 18th century the manor-house was enlarged palatially. As from 1760 Essling was imperial property. Behind the estate, in the open fields, is a mighty 18th century three-storey granary, the object of

protracted fighting during the Battle of Aspern.

Kagran was mentioned as "Chagaran" in around 1200. The existing Parish Church was built after the flooding in 1438. Despite being rebuilt many times, St. George's is still a simple little village church.

The fishing village of Stadlau was situated on a strip of land on the river and it held ferrying rights. In 1438 the village and the church were almost completely destroyed and then rebuilt further to the east.

The riverside settlement of Kaisermühlen was first mentioned in 1674 and belonged to Stadlau. After the course of the river was regulated — formerly the village lay on the right bank of the main branch of the Danube — the ship mills moved to the Freudenau and the steamship landing stage was transferred to the city side near the site of the future Reichsbrücke. The old settlement vanished and was replaced by large apartment houses. Between 1887 and 1895 Viktor Luntz' triple-aisled basilica was erected on the Schüttauplatz of today. In 1907 the Municipality of Vienna took over and enlarged Gänsehäufel bathing centre. The Donaupark with its 252 m. tower and other attractions was laid out on the occasion of the International Garden Display in 1964 in the water meadows between the Bruckhaufen estate and Wagramer Strasse. In 1973 work started on the International Centre, or UNO-City, planned by Johann Staber, and the Viennese International Conference Centre. The underground railway ensures speedy connections with all districts. A modern district centre quickly developed along the Wagramer Strasse where there are administrative offices, schools, social and medical facilities and extensive shopping amenties. The trend has been set and in future the city will certainly extend further on the other bank of the Danube.

a

b

a) Reichsbrücke
b) UNO City

c) View from the
Leopoldsberg across the
Danube and the New
Danube to the UNO City
and the Danube Tower

a) 22, Essling, Simonsgasse:
baroque granary bearing
traces of the struggles of
1809
b) 22, Aspern, Helden-
platz: Anton Fernkorn's
Lion of Aspern
c) 21, Stammersdorf

Early spring at the
Gänsehäufel on the Old
Danube

Page 150/151:
On the Old Danube